BIG TIME BUCK WHITE

BIG TIME BUCK WHITE

BY JOSEPH DOLAN TUOTTI

GROVE PRESS, INC., NEW YORK

Big Time Buck White *was first performed at Budd Schulberg's Writers Workshop in Watts, Los Angeles. The New York première took place on December 8, 1968 at the Village South Theatre. Produced by Zev Bufman, sets by Edward Burbridge, lighting by Thomas Skelton, costumes by Sara Brook. The play was directed by Dick Williams, with the following cast:*

HUNTER	Kirk Kirksey
HONEY MAN	David Moody
WEASEL	Van Kirksey
RUBBER BAND	Arnold Williams
JIVE	Ron Rich
WHITEY	Roger Klier
BIG TIME BUCK WHITE	Dick Williams

The play is set in the meeting hall of the Beautiful Alleluiah Days Organization. In the center of the stage, toward the back, there is a platformed podium, to the left of which is a trash can. Behind the podium, on the back wall, there is a door leading offstage. There is a desk and a chair against the stage right wall. Another trash can and a broom are against the wall behind the desk. A bulletin board is on the wall above the desk. Right and left center stage there are some connected folding chairs, the type found in many high school auditoriums. Signs are glued to the walls of both the stage and the auditorium, proclaiming RECRUIT; ARE YOUR DUES PAID; DON'T CHEW NO GUM; POLICE SIT UP FRONT; SAVE OUR UNCLE TOMS; BLACK CAN BE A BOMB; POLICE ARE PIGS; DON'T SMOKE NO DOPE (IN THE MEETING HALL); *On the back wall, a sign says:* WIPE OUT: BLEACH CREAMS, PROCESS HEADS, GAS-HEADS, KONKS, DO-RAGS, WHITE TALKING, WHITE THINKING, WHITE ACTING, AND WHITE WOMEN. *The stage looks like an abandoned schoolroom, complete with bookcases and a blackboard, on which is written* BLACK IS.

The place looks like a disaster area. There is trash, beer cans, wine bottles, food all over the

1

*place; the furniture is scattered across the room.
Last night was obviously a party night.*

As the play opens, we see HUNTER *asleep on one
of the benches.*

HONEY MAN *is in the lobby of the theater, having
an argument with someone. The door opens.* HONEY
MAN *enters, checks door to make sure it's locked,
and walks into audience.*

HONEY MAN: Wow. Look at this—you know now,
this is a shame. All you people come here to
be threatened. Don't you people know you're
in trouble? You can't go nowhere; the door's
locked. I just locked it myself. And the phone
don't work. You came here, and that's where
you made your mistake. Y'all came here to
watch Big Time and the Boys work out. (*He
moves onto stage, and starts picking up trash,
depositing some in trash can.*) That's precisely
what we are going to do. But there are some
rules. There are some rules that must be fol-
lowed closely . . . like . . . Big Time is
goin' to answer all your questions. But before
he does, you're goin' to have to "tap that
plate." Now that means you got to dig down
deep in your pockets and come up with all
your change. 'Cause we're goin' to be out
there with our "donation plate" and if you

don't "donate" you're goin' to be in even more trouble. You're goin' to be embarrassed. Big Time should be here in about fifteen minutes, just blowing your minds with a whole lot-a-soul. There are the Organizers, too. There's Weasel, and there's The Hunter. There's Rubber Band. Then there's Jive. There's Big Time, of course, and there's me. Now my name is Honey Man. Hon-ee Maann. My name was designed to make you feel at ease. So, just sit back and I'm goin' to tell you what it's all about. —We belong to an organization called BAD. B-A-D. Now BAD means Beautiful Alleluiah Days. We're an integraded social group. We first came upon the idea when Congress started giving all those other groups money. Our theme is "innerism." You got to go to innerism. And also, you must be pov-er-ty-stricken. Now all of us aren't, 'cause if we were, we wouldn't be integraded. Now see if you can dig that. That's just about the way it is, really.

WEASEL (*enters*): Heyyy!

HONEY MAN (*filling Weasel's hand with trash*): Hey, Weasel!

WEASEL (*deposits trash in can*): How ya doin', Honey Man? Everything cool, Man?

HONEY MAN: Where's Jive, Man?

3

WEASEL: Oh, Jive'll be here, Man.

HONEY MAN: Is he still mad?

WEASEL: Mad? Man, that cat is nasty-eeeeeee! (*Walks down to desk.*)

HONEY MAN: He's been like that ever since that party last night.

WEASEL: No lie. Hey, I see you got some nice folks out there.

HONEY MAN: Yeah.

WEASEL: Are they ready for Jive, Honey Man? 'Cause that Jive is goin' to be somethin' else tonight.

HONEY MAN: Considering the fact that he thinks that we started all that rioting at that last party and we might lose all that poverty money. And you know that BAD is his baby. And knowin' he knows all that, you know he's goin' to come here wanting to kick somebody's ass, Weasel. I just hope he don't start on me . . . So what you do, Weasel, is you take this broom, and git to sweeping this floor, all right? (*Puts broom in Weasel's hand.*)

WEASEL: You better tell that sucker where it's at, Man. I think you're afraid of the cat, Honey Man. (*Starts to sweep.*)

HONEY MAN: I ain't scared of nobody, Weasel. But I got to eat, Man. Come help me with this bench, so I don't wake up The Hunter again.

WEASEL: You better believe that as long as Jive's in charge you won't be eatin' too long.

HONEY MAN: Yeah.

WEASEL: Man, as long as that cat's been in charge, we should be as big as the N. Double A. C. P. But as it is, we only got half membership goin' for us, and half of them is Brothers. And you know ain't no Brother goin' to pay his dues. I never met a cat who's suppose to be from the street who couldn't handle "Whitey" 'til I met Jive.

HONEY MAN: Now wait a damn minute, Weasel. You can't be talkin' about Jive like that.

WEASEL: Hey, Man, ninety-five per cent of those people don't want to be here, Honey Man. Ninety-five per cent of those people are fakin' they're liberals or something. And that, plus what happened to that so-called honored guest, is why that party turned into a full-scale riot.

HONEY MAN *and* WEASEL *sit on either end of Hunter's bench and, during the following conversation, bounce the bench up*

5

and down, shaking up HUNTER, *who is still asleep.*

HONEY MAN: You can't be blaming all that terror on Jive, Man.

WEASEL: Who the Hell do you think invited that cat, Man?

HONEY MAN: Hey, can't no one cat start nothin' that big.

WEASEL: Well, you can't blame it on the rest of us.

HONEY MAN: Hell, yes!

WEASEL: Hell, no!

HONEY MAN: Hell, yes!

WEASEL: Hell, no!

HONEY MAN: Weasel, somebody put somethin' in that cat's drink, Man.

WEASEL: What you looking at me for?

HONEY MAN: It had to be one of the Organizers.

WEASEL: I don't know who it was, but whoever it was sure started some wild shit, didn't he?

HONEY MAN (*lifts the bench, almost dumping* HUNTER *on floor.* HUNTER *indignantly gets up, walks to the other bench, and deposits himself there*): Yeah.

6

WEASEL: Hey, Honey Man, did Jive ever find out who did it?

HONEY MAN: Not only does he know, Man, but somebody told me he got proof. (*He continues straightening up.*)

WEASEL (*goes back to sweeping*): Honey Man, I'm surprised at you, Brother. I'm surprised you ain't been able to see all the changes that cat's been goin' through. Now you know I got a very deep perception of people. I been watching that cat and I've been watching him closely, Man. That cat's been goin' through a whole lot of changes. You can't keep up with the changes just watching the changes he's been changin' into.

HONEY MAN: Like what changes you talking about, Weasel?

WEASEL: I'm talking about the general overall changes. That's why I been doin' what the rest of the Boys have asked me to do. I've been taking a look at the situation that BAD is in, and I'm making a move that we all get together and vote that sucker down.

HONEY MAN: Like what boys are you talking about, Weasel?

WEASEL: Our Boys.

7

HONEY MAN: Which ones?

WEASEL: You know I can't mention no names.

HONEY MAN (*snatches broom from* WEASEL): Well, damn, Weasel.

WEASEL: Hey, Man, forget about that party, Brother. Last week Jive goes ahead and announces that BAD is starting a new class.

HONEY MAN: Uh huh.

WEASEL: Now he calls this class "The Future Ethnic Behavior Pattern of the Afro-American in Relationship to His Present Awareness of Ghetto Expansion and the Imminent Growth of Other Problems" . . . Teacher, Jive. Hey, you know I had to go to this class. When I walked into this class, here's Jive standing before the group, and he was talking to this big Italian cat. And he said, "I don't care how bad Ty Cobb was, Maury Wills was better, and I can prove it." And this little Brother in the back stands up and says, "I got proof! I got proof! Christopher Columbus was a racist." And another Brother says, "So was his Mama." And this big cat stood up. And he said, "I got proof." He said, "Christopher Columbus did not discover America. It was discovered by an African Prince by the name of Prince Willie

8

Sheldon who came over here in a Cadillac a long time before ol' Chris was even born." Which is probably true, come to think of it.

HONEY MAN: Yeah.

WEASEL: But the point is, Jive ain't taking care of no business, Baby, and I'm making a move that we all get together and vote that sucker down and out.

HONEY MAN: I believe you're a damn liar, Weasel.

WEASEL: A what, Man?

HONEY MAN: I think you're trying to psych me out or somethin', Man.

WEASEL: Honey Man, you know I don't play that signifyin' stuff, Man.

HONEY MAN: I ain't signifying nothing, Weasel.

WEASEL: And you know I don't play that lying jazz, Man.

HONEY MAN: Well, I know to vote you have to be an Organizer.

WEASEL: I know that.

HONEY MAN: There ain't but five Organizers in BAD.

WEASEL: I know that.

9

HONEY MAN (*starts to dust the bench*): Now I know you don't have Jive's vote, and Big Time can't vote. You don't have Rubber Band's vote.

WEASEL: Hey, Man . . . me and Rubber Band is tight.

HONEY MAN: You don't have The Hunter's vote.

WEASEL: Me and The Hunter's together, too.

HONEY MAN: Hell, Hunter wouldn't be here if it wasn't for me.

WEASEL: Oh, well, I know that.

HONEY MAN: Well, you don't have Jive's vote, and you don't have Big Time's vote, and you don't have Rubber Band's vote, and you don't have . . .

WEASEL: Hey, don't tell me whose vote I don't have, Man! I know who I'm voting for.

HONEY MAN: Well, damn, Weasel, that makes *one*, Baby.

WEASEL: Well, I'll just have to go to the power of voting, Honey Man. (*Takes out wallet. Starts to finger the money.*) The Power of Voting. Here's my man Rubber Band's *Vote*; here's The Hunter's *Vote*; hey, here's Jive's *Vote*; hey, here's yours. (*He moves around the bench and tempts* HONEY MAN *with the money.*)

10

HONEY MAN (*avoids the money, and keeps dusting*): Not me, Man. Uh, uh, not me.

WEASEL: Oh?

HONEY MAN (*moves toward* WEASEL): Not me, uh uh . . . (*He eyes the money.*) Well, I might, Man! You know.

WEASEL: You damn right you "might," Man. Without me, you cats would be back there in them alleys, bankrupt, where you was when we started.

HONEY MAN: Well, what I'll do is . . . I'll give it some kind of serious thought. Come on, we should all get together in a group . . . get us somethin' . . .

WEASEL: Like a bottle of wine?

HONEY MAN: Yeah, with a bottle of wine, you know . . .

WEASEL: And some freaks?

HONEY MAN: Some freaks. And discuss . . . it . . .

HONEY MAN *and* WEASEL: Intelligently. Yeah. (*They chuckle.*)

WEASEL: Did you hear about Rubber Band?

HONEY MAN: Rubber Band?

11

WEASEL: Yeah, Rubber Band.

HONEY MAN: No. What happened to Rubber Band?

WEASEL: You jivin'?

HONEY MAN: No, what happened to Rubber Band?

WEASEL: Where you been?

HONEY MAN: Out there.

WEASEL: You been high.

HONEY MAN: Well, what happened to Rubber Band?

WEASEL: You'd better get yourself together.

HONEY MAN: So . . . What happened to Rubber Band?

WEASEL: Well, would you believe . . .

HUNTER (*waking up*): HONEY MAN! BABY!

HONEY MAN: The Hunter!

WEASEL: Hey, Hunter. How ya doin'?

HONEY MAN: Have you got a good one to tell?

HUNTER: Ain't I?!

WEASEL: Ain't he!

HONEY MAN: What happened?

Through all this HUNTER *keeps trying to*

push WEASEL *out of the conversation.*
WEASEL *keeps trying to jump back in the
middle.*

HUNTER: The cops threw Rubber Band in the crazy
house, into the Psychiatric Ward, Baby.

HONEY MAN: In the what? . . . What did he do?

WEASEL: In the Happy-Dale, Baby.

HUNTER: It was like Bellevue, Honey Man.

HONEY MAN: Well, what did he do?

HUNTER: What *didn't* he do! Honey Man, remember
that party last night?

HONEY MAN: Yeah.

HUNTER: That turned out to be so disorganized?

HONEY MAN: Yeah.

HUNTER: Well, you remember how drunk Rubber
Band got?

HONEY MAN: Yeah, he was tore up.

HUNTER: Tore up? He was wiped *out!* Rubber Band
came out of that party . . .

HUNTER *and* WEASEL: He was crossin' the street.
He got hit by a moving car.

WEASEL: He got knocked into a street sewer.

13

HUNTER (*pushes* WEASEL): Don't tell my tale, Weasel!

They push and bump each other.

WEASEL: Hey, Hunter, I was telling that tale, Man. I was telling that tale.

HUNTER: You're not telling My Tale.

WEASEL: I was telling that tale!

HUNTER: Nobody tells My Tale!

WEASEL: I was telling that tale, Man. I was telling that tale.

HONEY MAN (*he moves in between them, attempting to separate them*): Hush up! Be quiet, Weasel! Shut up! Will you shut up?

HUNTER: Nobody tells My Tale. Don't tell My Tale! . . .

WEASEL: Wait a minute. I was telling that tale. I was telling that tale! . . .

HUNTER: Nobody tells My Tale. You're not telling My Tale, nobody tells My Tale. Don't tell My Tale! . . .

WEASEL: Hey, Man, I was telling that tale. I was telling that tale when you woke up! . . .

HONEY MAN (*to* WEASEL): Will you shut up? I

mean HUSH! I mean it, Man. Shut up! Shut up, Man, shut up. SHUT UP!

HUNTER: NOBODY DOES MY THING!

HONEY MAN: Now, let the man do his thing. Come on and do your thing. O.K., Hunter?

HUNTER: It was just like Weasel said, Honey Man. Rubber Band came out of that party, Baby. He was wiped out. He was crossing the street, Honey Man. He got hit by a moving car and got knocked into a street sewer . . .

HONEY MAN: Into the street sewer?

HUNTER: Baby, he had mud poppin' all off his body, lookin' like a damn water fountain statue—inside a street sewer.

HONEY MAN: Inside a street sewer!

WEASEL: Yeah, Honey Man. That sucker was standing in mud . . .

HUNTER *and* WEASEL: . . . clear up to his Natural.

HUNTER: He was funkyyyy!

HUNTER *and* WEASEL: Whhoooeeeee!

RUBBER BAND *enters from the back of the auditorium and moves down the aisle.*

RUBBER BAND: . . . ANKLES, MAN! . . . (*Moves*

toward HUNTER, *menacingly*.) . . . I went up to my ankles, Man.

HUNTER (*in a loud whisper to* HONEY MAN, *teasing* RUBBER BAND): Smelled so bad . . . funked up the whole block . . .

RUBBER BAND: My ankles, Sucker . . .

HUNTER: Lie! Lie! Lie!

RUBBER BAND: Hey, Hunter, you're too small to be messing with me, don't you know that, Jack?

HUNTER: Don't tell me it wasn't up to your Natural, Baby.

RUBBER BAND (*follows* HUNTER, *threatening him*): I'll knock you upside your head, Hunter . . .

HUNTER: Big Time saw the fuzz pull you out . . .

ALL: Whhooooeeeeee . . .

HONEY MAN (*stepping between them*): Rubber Band, The Hunter's done wiped you out!

RUBBER BAND: Yeah . . . you come close here, Sucker, and we'll see who gets wiped out . . .

HUNTER: Rubber Band, get in your corner . . .

RUBBER BAND *goes after* HUNTER; *he's restrained by* WEASEL *and* HONEY MAN.

16

WEASEL *and* HONEY MAN: Hey, Man! . . . Hey, wait . . . Hey, wait. No, no.

WEASEL: He's just mad 'cause he got all those fines to pay.

RUBBER BAND *takes trash can off through door at back of stage.*

HUNTER: FINES! . . . Honey Man, did you ever get your lips caught in a pop bottle, Brother?

HONEY MAN: Yeah. Yeah. Yeah.

HUNTER: Police pulled him out of that sewer . . . the mud was sucking from his Natural through his shades . . . down his face, his chest, his bow legs; he was standing there naked . . . and still drunk.

HONEY MAN: What did the fuzz do, Man?

WEASEL: Fined him . . . Fined him bad, Man!

HUNTER: Rubber Band got fined for indecent exposure, being drunk, disturbing the peace, and . . .

WEASEL: Possession!

HUNTER *and* WEASEL: And they got him for being naked!

All laugh out loud. RUBBER BAND *makes noises from the back room.*

17

WEASEL: Then they went upside his head . . .

HUNTER: . . . after they threw him in the "loony ward" . . .

WEASEL: . . . after they went upside his head . . .

HUNTER: . . . with not one . . .

WEASEL: . . . but two guns . . .

HUNTER: . . . Whop! . . . Whop!

They all break up.

HONEY MAN: What did they hit him for? . . .

HUNTER: The fool was screaming *Police brutality! Police brutality!* in a white neighborhood.

They all laugh again.

RUBBER BAND (*comes back in, threatening* WEASEL *with trash can*): Hey, Weasel . . . What do you think you're doin', huh, Sucker?

WEASEL (*moves out of the way*): Who, me?

Through the following exchange, RUBBER BAND *chases* WEASEL *with the trash can.* HONEY MAN *is busy sweeping, trying to stay between them.*

RUBBER BAND: That's right . . . we're suppose to be together . . .

18

WEASEL: What do you mean, "What am I doin'?"

RUBBER BAND: Are we together here, Man, or what?

WEASEL: We're together . . .

RUBBER BAND: Then what you testing me for, huh, Sucker?

WEASEL: I ain't testin' nobody.

RUBBER BAND: Shit . . . that's what it looks like, Man; getting your rocks off listenin' to that silly fool over there, you know that, Jack?

HONEY MAN *gets trash can away from* RUBBER BAND.

WEASEL: Hey, Brother, what are you getting so defensive about?

RUBBER BAND: What do you mean, "defensive," huh?

WEASEL: You're asking me what I'm doin'. I'm havin' fun. Ain't no big thing.

RUBBER BAND (*walks up to podium*): You better watch yourself; you hear that, Jack?

HUNTER (*grabs his hat and jacket; starts to leave*): I came here to do My Thing, Baby. Each one of you got Your Thing to do. Honey Man, if you don't want to hear it, fa-get-it!

19

HONEY MAN: What is the matter with you, Hunter?

WEASEL: Hey, Man. Wait a minute . . .

HONEY MAN *and* WEASEL (*restraining* HUNTER): What's the matter . . . wait a minute, Hunter . . .

WEASEL: What are you getting so defensive about?

HONEY MAN: Where you come up with all this paranoia all of a sudden?

WEASEL: Why all of a sudden you gettin' . . . (*Reacting to* HONEY MAN.) Para—*who*?

HONEY MAN: PARA—*NOIA*

They all laugh.

HUNTER: Fa-get-it!

HUNTER *tries to leave. They hold him.*

HONEY MAN: What's the matter with you, Hunter? Calm down . . . calm down.

WEASEL: What happened? Tell the man . . .

HONEY MAN: What happened to the fool?

HUNTER: He don't want to hear it, Weasel.

HONEY MAN: What happened to the fool, Man?

WEASEL: Tell the man your tale.

They give HUNTER *the floor.*

HONEY MAN: What happened?

HUNTER (*acts it out grandly*): Honey Man . . . Jive goes down to get him out. Finds Rubber Band, our Number One Black Militant, and some goofy white priest in a corner, hummin' church hymns.

HONEY MAN: Church hymns!

HUNTER *nods and sits, chin on hands, humming "Rock of Ages."*

RUBBER BAND (*approaches menacingly*): You know, Weasel, you ain't showin' me nothin', Sucker. Are you hep to that, Jack? Huh?

WEASEL (*evading* RUBBER BAND): Well, you ain't showin' me too much, either, Jack.

RUBBER BAND: Maybe you think I'm some kind of sure thing, huh, Jack?

HONEY MAN: Say, Rubber Band, why don't you just come on down and fight the man, Man?

HONEY MAN *shoves* RUBBER BAND *into* WEASEL.

RUBBER BAND *and* WEASEL: Hey! Hey! Hey, Man! What you doin'? Hey. Hey . . .

WEASEL: Hey, Man. Don't you go startin' nothin', Man. Say, he's not uptight about that; he's uptight about somethin' else.

21

RUBBER BAND: Don't you tell me what I'm uptight about, Brother. I know what I'm uptight about. You hep to that, huh?

WEASEL: Hey, Brother, if you ain't so uptight, you're mighty defensive about somethin' you shouldn't be defensive about.

RUBBER BAND: Sucker, if you say "defensive" one more time, I'll kick dents in your head big as watermelons, get that, Sucker?

WEASEL: Shit . . . hey . . . what you doin' . . . hey . . . hey . . . We're together here, Man . . . we're together . . . I'm with you . . . you with me . . . it ain't no big thing . . .

HUNTER: Well, y'all don't sound like y'all got y'all-selves together to me.

HONEY MAN: Hunter, don't you know that this is some kind of classified secret plot to get Jive's job, Man?

HUNTER: Oh?

HONEY MAN: Yeah.

WEASEL: Hey, Brother, you know I'm a business-man. As soon as Jive gets here we'll vote the sucker down and we'll take over this organization.

22

HONEY MAN: They sure make an interesting pair of spies, don't they?

HUNTER: Honey Man, I came here to tell you a tale.

HONEY MAN: Now come here, Hunter, come here . . .

HUNTER: One more time . . .

HONEY MAN: What happened to the fool, really . . .

HUNTER: Honey Man, I'm not going to do it but *one more time!*

HONEY MAN: What happened?

RUBBER BAND: You better be cool, Sucker.

They give HUNTER the floor.

HUNTER (*acts it out again*): Jive goes down to get him out, and finds him and that goofy white priest sittin' in that corner hummin' them church hymns . . . (HUNTER *sits down, chin in hands, humming "Rock of Ages."*) Honey Man, this goofy white priest, he stands up, looks at Jive and says, "Rubber Band is going to be our next Pope." Rubber Band is still in the corner, hummin'. (HUNTER *hums a few more bars of "Rock of Ages."*) Rubber Band looks up at Jive and says, "Integration ain't bad, Brother." (HUNTER *hums a few more bars of "Rock of Ages."*)

23

HONEY MAN: So what did Jive do?

HUNTER: Jive looked at him and said, "That fool belongs." Jive left him there.

RUBBER BAND: Hunter, you know, you have to be lucky I'm not on top of this scene. You know that, Brother?

HONEY MAN: Would you look at this fool.

HUNTER: . . . Like he had somethin' to say . . .

RUBBER BAND (*to* HUNTER): Look here, Man. I told you you're too small to be messing with me, Man.

HUNTER: Don't tell it to me. Tell it to them, "Big Time Rubber Band."

HONEY MAN: What's he goin' to say if he can't curse, huh, Man?

HUNTER: Not a damn thing.

RUBBER BAND (*goes after* HUNTER): Shit! . . . I'll beat you upside your head.

He is blocked by HONEY MAN *and* WEASEL.

WEASEL: Hey, Brother . . . hey . . . hey . . . Brother . . .

HUNTER: Imagine if Rubber Band had Jive's gig!

HONEY MAN: Uh uh. Uh uh.

24

HUNTER: Uh uh . . . fa-get-it.

HONEY MAN: You hip to it?

RUBBER BAND (*turning on* HONEY MAN): Honey Man, Brother, you been trying to get Jive's job ever since BAD started, Sucker . . . who you kiddin'? Huh, Jack?

HONEY MAN: What?

HUNTER: That happens to be true, Honey Man. I know you lookin' for Jive's gig, Baby.

HONEY MAN: Oh WOW, Man.

RUBBER BAND: "Oh WOW"—What do you mean, "Oh WOW," Sucker?

HUNTER: That's true, Baby.

HONEY MAN: Hunter, don't tell me you got yourself mixed up in this half-assed intrigue thing they got goin' here, Man?

HUNTER: Not really, Honey Man. Weasel, we ain't talked price yet.

WEASEL: Well, I'll give ya money now! (*Gives* HUNTER *some money.*)

HUNTER: I want some more!

HONEY MAN: Hunter, you better remember who found you in the streets . . .

HUNTER: WHAT!

HONEY MAN: Who found you in the street? Who picked you up when you were down, who fed you, who's the cause of you bein' here, WHO FOUND YOU IN THE STREET?

HUNTER: HONEY MAN, DON'T YOU EVER CALL SUNSET BOULEVARD NO "STREET"!

WEASEL: *Sunset Boulevard?*

All laugh, except HONEY MAN.

HUNTER: North Beverly Hills, Baby! . . . There I am, walking with some of the finest people I know, in my new African dashiki. And you know I'm lookin' goooooooood. I'm walkin' and talkin', sayin', "How do you do? How are you?," and there he is, lookin' like he's lookin' . . . only *funkier!* I thought he was goin' to ask me for some carefare back to Watts . . . instead, he leans over. He says, "I'm Honey Man. I got a poverty gig here I want you to belong to" . . . Weasel, he even hands me a brochure. He looks me up and down and says, "Our organization needs . . . uh . . . class."

All laugh, except HONEY MAN.

HUNTER (*walks over to* WEASEL *and puts his arm*

around WEASEL's *shoulder*): Well, shit, that's why I'm here. To bring *class* . . .

All break up.

WEASEL: Speakin' of class, you know I just came from the mint . . .

HUNTER: From the mint!

WEASEL: I got some money here that ain't been spent yet, damn right. Ol' Abe is still grinnin' . . . and if you don't mind, you know I'd like to give you some . . .

HUNTER: Well, you know I don't mind.

RUBBER BAND *rushes in, snatches wallet, goes up on podium.* WEASEL *goes after his money.*

WEASEL: You better give me my wallet back.

RUBBER BAND (*crosses to other side of podium*): Don't go givin' that little sucker none of your bread, Man.

WEASEL: You better give me my wallet back.

RUBBER BAND: Aw naw . . .

RUBBER BAND *is on the podium.* WEASEL *is standing on the floor.* RUBBER BAND *waves the money and* WEASEL *jumps for it. Intermixed argument.*

27

WEASEL *and* RUBBER BAND: You better give me
back my wallet . . . Wait a minute . . .
You better give me back my money . . . You
can't do that . . . You better give me back
my dough . . . Naw uh uh . . . You better
give me back my wallet, Man . . . What's
wrong with you, Man? . . . You better give
me back my wallet, Man . . .

RUBBER BAND: That little sucker will turn you on,
Brother.

WEASEL: Give me my wallet.

RUBBER BAND: This sucker will trick you, Brother.
He will trick you.

WEASEL: Give me my dough, Man.

RUBBER BAND: You must be losin' your mind!

HUNTER: He wouldn't take my money!

> HONEY MAN *comes up behind* RUBBER
> BAND, *snatches wallet, moves down to the
> desk.*

RUBBER BAND: What you doin', Man?

HONEY MAN (*exploring wallet*): Ooooweee, with
all this money, what you doin' on the poverty
scene, Baby?

HUNTER: Oooooooooo-ooooooo!

28

WEASEL: You don't know nothin' about my gig, Sucker!

HUNTER: Weasel, as rich as you are . . .

WEASEL: You don't know nothin' about my gig, either.

HONEY MAN: You got enough money there to buy Sears.

WEASEL: What do you know about my gig?

HUNTER: Now we know you *got* one.

RUBBER BAND: Sure he does.

WEASEL: Oh. All of a sudden I'm the bad guy, huh.

ALL: Yeah.

HUNTER: This sucker lives in Hollywood Hills!

HONEY MAN: Yeah.

HUNTER: . . . Wears Tyrone Power clothes . . .

HONEY MAN: Yeah.

WEASEL: How come all of a sudden I'm the bad guy?

HUNTER: . . . And drives a 1958 fish-tail . . . Cadillac . . .

HONEY MAN: Yeah.

RUBBER BAND *sneaks down, snatches wal-*

29

let again, and goes back up to podium,
fingering the money.

RUBBER BAND: Affluent, bourgeois, upper-middle
class Sucker! What you gettin' so "defensive"
about, Brother?

WEASEL (*charges up and grabs money back, moves*
away from them, counting it): "Defensive?"
Hey, Man, don't ever call me "defensive,"
that's not where I am at. I just got some good
stuff from Acapulco. You don't get any.

RUBBER BAND: Hey, Brother. Wait a minute,
Man . . .

HUNTER (*goes where the money is; "makes friends"*
with WEASEL): Ah, Rubber Band, I think you
just cut yourself off.

RUBBER BAND: Hey, Brother . . . We're suppose
to be together, Man.

WEASEL: Well, we're together, Man . . . but don't
call me defensive, that ain't where I'm at.

RUBBER BAND: O.K., Brother. I'm hep to it. Shit,
put it to me.

HUNTER: Put it to him . . .

RUBBER BAND: That's right. Put it to me, Jack . . .

HONEY MAN: Like you better get your ass off this

30

podium before Jive puts it to you, Man . . . Jive don't want nobody on this podium except Big Time . . . So before I end up gettin' in trouble, just get your ass off . . .

WEASEL: Stay up there, Rubber Band.

HONEY MAN (*goes after* WEASEL): Let me get somethin' straight with you, Weasel, before you go ahead with this grand coup-type thing you got goin' here . . .

WEASEL (*confronts him*): It's called politics, Honey Man . . . Pol-E-tics . . .

HONEY MAN: Before you go doin' any more politickin' . . . just remember I'm next in line for Jive's job, Baby.

WEASEL: Who is?

HONEY MAN: I am. Me. I'm Jive's right-hand man . . .

RUBBER BAND: And that's the one I'm goin' to cut off too, Sucker.

HONEY MAN (*turns on* RUBBER BAND, *almost running over* HUNTER): What'd ya say, Man?

HUNTER: You heard what he said . . .

HONEY MAN: You cats remember, you can only vote *in,* not *out.*

31

ALL: Ohhh?? Ohhhhh . . .

RUBBER BAND (*to* HONEY MAN): Man, you don't have enough experience in the street to get Jive's job, Jack.

HONEY MAN: Who don't?!

ALL: You don't!!

HUNTER: Honey Man, you too fine to come from the streets.

HONEY MAN: Hunter, you must be out of your cotton pickin' mind, sayin' somethin' like that . . .

RUBBER BAND: Hey, Brother . . . I must be out of my cotton pickin' mind too, huh, Jack? . . . (*He pretends to take out a switchblade, dives for* HONEY MAN, *cutting at his head.*) What you gonna do about it, huh, Sucker? . . .

HONEY MAN *wheels, catches* RUBBER BAND *with an imaginary gun, sticks it in his back, braces him up, and walks him to the center of the room.*

WEASEL: Hey, Honey Man?

HONEY MAN: What?

WEASEL: Did you ever shoot a gun before?

HONEY MAN: Uh . . . I know how to pull a trigger . . .

32

WEASEL: But you ain't never *used* one?

HONEY MAN: No. I ain't shot nobody in my life.

HUNTER: What you're saying is that you ain't no Billy the Kid.

HONEY MAN: No, I'm a Honey Man.

WEASEL: Well, if you ain't no Billy the Kid, you sure as hell goin' to die like one.

All draw imaginary guns on HONEY MAN.

HONEY MAN (*Points gun straight up, looks at it, smiles, then puts it in his pocket*): Uh . . . I think you cats are trying to tell me somethin'.

ALL: That's right. It's called *Black Power*, Sucker! Ooooooo! (*All laugh, put guns away, get together, enjoying it all.*)

JIVE (*enters from back of the auditorium, moves down through audience and onto the stage. He's in a hurry. When the others see him they try to get themselves organized.* HUNTER *and* HONEY MAN *move desk and chair in front of the podium*): *Honey Man!* Is this what the hell you call takin' care of business, huh? Is this what you call taking care of business? Look at all these people out here. Instead of taking care of business, you just . . . (*Takes a long look at* RUBBER BAND's *rear end.* RUBBER BAND *is very busy polishing the podium*.) Negro, are you out of your mind? Get off this damn podium! Get off of the podium and stay off the podium . . .

WEASEL: Stay up there, Rubber Band.

JIVE (*goes after* WEASEL): Look, I'll bust you right in your mouth.

WEASEL (*evades* JIVE): Hey, Man, stop trying to be so mean.

JIVE (*moves to his desk*): "*Trying* to be so mean" . . . I'm so mean, it gets me upset just thinking about it.

RUBBER BAND: Ah, Man, why don't you come on, huh, Jive?

JIVE: Oh, don't you say nothin' 'cause the way I feel about you I could bite into your head and kill you.

HUNTER (*real swish*): Oh, Jive, now come on . . .

JIVE: *Ah, shut up!* You wouldn't even make a good faggot, you telling me something!

HONEY MAN: All right! All right! All right!

JIVE: I'm sick of you, you big dummy. People show up here and you people here got to go ahead displaying all your "Niggerisms."

ALL: "NIGGERISMS!!"

JIVE: Niggerisms. After today you don't work no more; you ain't nothing but a bunch of low-class spooks anyway. Give me a count, Honey Man, before I lose my temper.

HONEY MAN (*starts to count the audience*): One . . . yeah . . . two . . . three . . . you're four . . . five . . . six, six . . . seven . . . that's eight . . . uh, nine . . . you're ten, yeah . . .

JIVE: Honey Man.

HONEY MAN: . . . You're eleven . . .

JIVE: You're fired.

HONEY MAN: Hey, Jive.

JIVE: YOU'RE FIRED!!

WEASEL: Hey, Man, what you doin' firin' Honey Man?

JIVE: Because he's suppose to be taking care of the house while I'm gone. Instead, he lets a bunch of wild nuts run around here disrupting everything.

RUBBER BAND (*to* HONEY MAN): This sucker is puttin' you down, Brother . . .

WEASEL: . . . You're his right-hand man, Man.

RUBBER BAND: . . . You oughta go over there and jam your head between his lips, Man.

JIVE (*to* RUBBER BAND): You know, you sure would look funny all bow-legged and without no head.

RUBBER BAND: Hey, Man, I ain't afraid, Jack.

JIVE: Unless you got nine lives, you'd better be . . .

RUBBER BAND (*to* JIVE): I don't see no whiskers in your cheeks!

JIVE: Well, you will see some whiskers if you . . .

HUNTER: Why do we got to fight all the time, huh? Why can't we get along?

RUBBER BAND: The sucker is prejudiced, Hunter.

HUNTER: Prejudiced?

WEASEL (*to* JIVE): You know how them high yellows are!!

JIVE: Shut up. You got people here I don't even know. What's he doin' here? Hunter, what are you doin' here? You ain't no Organizer.

HUNTER: I been doin' it, Jive.

JIVE: No you haven't.

HUNTER: I been on the payroll.

JIVE: Since when?

HUNTER: Since the bee-ginning.

JIVE: Who gave you this job?

HUNTER (*looks around. After a long pause, he chooses* HONEY MAN): HONEY MAN!

JIVE: *What?* (*He goes to the door at back of stage and opens it.*)

HONEY MAN *tries to get to* HUNTER; RUBBER BAND *and* WEASEL *try to block him;* JIVE *tries to get him out.*

HONEY MAN (*to* HUNTER): You better hope they got a cure for rigamortis, Sucker! . . . 'Cause if they don't, I know some land crabs gonna be eatin' soul food tonight, Sucker! (*Follows* JIVE *out.*)

HUNTER: Honey Man, you can yell all you want to, Baby, because I'm splitting.

RUBBER BAND: Hey, Hunter!

RUBBER BAND *and* WEASEL: Wait a minute, Brother. Don't leave, Man. Hey, Hunter. Where ya goin', Brother?

HUNTER: I don't need this. I'm goin' back to the Post Office.

RUBBER BAND: Hey, I know you happenin', Hunter.

WEASEL: Sure he is.

HUNTER: Weasel, you got your hand on my dashiki.

WEASEL (*brushing* HUNTER'*s dashiki off*): Oh! I'm sorry, Brother. Ooooooooooo.

RUBBER BAND: Where did ya cop this cloth from, Hunter?

HUNTER: Ain't it too much?

RUBBER BAND: Oh, it's *together!*

HUNTER (*pulling himself together*): This is my nighttime attire.

RUBBER BAND: You got yourself together, Hunter!

HUNTER (*strutting around*): I can walk under the lights with this attire.

WEASEL: Yeah!

RUBBER BAND *and* WEASEL: Yeah!

RUBBER BAND: You got yourself together, Brother!

ALL: Yeah! Shit! Oh, yeah!

WEASEL: You know, Hunter . . . I'd . . . uh . . . like to pay your cleaning bill.

HUNTER: You know I don't mind.

RUBBER BAND: Give him a dolla'.

HUNTER: Hell no, Man. Cleaning went up.

RUBBER BAND: Hunter, why don't you stay and help Weasel and me out, Man?

HUNTER: Like . . . well . . . do I have to, Man?

RUBBER BAND: No, you really don't.

HUNTER (*needs more urging*): No, Rubber Band. You know I know I really don't.

RUBBER BAND: Yeah, but Weasel and me, we're getting ready to do our thing. You know.

HUNTER: Yeah.

RUBBER BAND: Yeah.

HUNTER: So.

RUBBER BAND: And if you don't . . . I'm goin' to rip the cloth off your behind, Brother.

HUNTER (*needs no more urging*): Rubber Band's BAD, huh?

WEASEL: Of course he's BAD.

HONEY MAN *and* JIVE *come back in.* HONEY MAN *straightens his tie.*

JIVE: . . . listen to it . . . And you better stay straight, Sucker!

HONEY MAN: Well, you are *the* boss on *the* white man's gig, Jive.

JIVE (*goes back to desk and sits down*): I know that. Just do your job, see. I know my job. These people here are out to make me lose some money . . . I don't know which one of them is behind it, but I do know one nigger who's not goin' to be here much longer . . . especially after what he did at that last party I gave . . . (*He fixes his gaze on* RUBBER BAND.)

HONEY MAN (*standing behind* JIVE'S *chair*): Well, let's take care of business . . .

RUBBER BAND: What you lookin' at me for, huh, Jack?

JIVE: 'Cause you're the one nigger I suspect that sabotaged the last party I gave . . .

WEASEL: Hey, Jive!

RUBBER BAND: Hey! Sabotage?

HUNTER: Oh! Come on!

JIVE: That's right. Sabotage.

WEASEL: Who you callin' NIGGER, NIGGER?

JIVE (*indicates* RUBBER BAND): That NIGGER, NIGGER!

WEASEL: Honey Man . . .

JIVE: You leave Honey Man out of this.

RUBBER BAND: Hey, Man, why you accusing me of sabotagin' my own gig, huh, Sucker?

JIVE: *Your* gig?

RUBBER BAND: What's wrong with you, Jive?

JIVE: *MY GIG.*

RUBBER BAND: You must be losin' your mind! Shit!

WEASEL: Hey, Man, you can call them niggers "niggers" . . . but don't call *me* no nigger. I'm a businessman . . . I could be out there making some money for this Organization, Jive. I don't have to come here and be called no nig . . .

JIVE (*stands up, towering over* WEASEL): *Shut up,* before I rip your hips off and make you eat 'em.

WEASEL: I quit, Man.

JIVE (*sits back down*): Good.

RUBBER BAND: Hey, Man . . . Hey, Brother . . .

WEASEL: Hey, Man, this cat is threatenin' bodily harm . . .

HUNTER (*starts to leave*): And you know, I don't want no harm done to my body!

They grab him and bring him back.

41

WEASEL: Hunter, he don't have no business threatening nobody.

HUNTER: No, he ain't got no . . .

WEASEL: . . . calling nobody no niggers, Man! You ain't got no business threatening me, Jive! I'm a businessman . . .

HONEY MAN: Weasel, don't you know, this man is bringin' up a serious charge against your man Rubber Band.

WEASEL: I know that.

RUBBER BAND: Well, let's see what the sucker's got to say, Man.

HUNTER: Yeah. Let's hear what he's got to say.

WEASEL: He ain't got no special privileges, Man.

JIVE: I got proof of what I'm sayin'.

RUBBER BAND: Wh . . . Whaa . . . What you mean you got proof?

JIVE (to RUBBER BAND): You're the one . . . you're the one who slipped that LSD pill to our honored guest, that grand duke I invited from down South.

RUBBER BAND: The cat blames it on a Brother, Man.

42

HUNTER (*in mock disbelief*): Oooooo!

RUBBER BAND: Did you see that, Man? He blames it on a Brother.

HUNTER: A Brother blaming another Brother.

RUBBER BAND: Ain't that too much!

HUNTER: Rubber Band, it's simple to me. He wants you out.

WEASEL: Best we vote him out.

RUBBER BAND: Honey Man, he didn't even think of blaming it on Whitey.

JIVE: Whitey didn't do it!

HUNTER: How do you know, Jive?

JIVE: Because it ain't something Whitey would do. It's only something a funny lookin' nut like that would do.

RUBBER BAND: Prove it, Sucker.

JIVE: I don't have to prove it. You did it.

HUNTER: Hey, Jive, don't you know that when Brothers get high, they think they can fly, Man?

RUBBER BAND: That's right, Man . . . LSD is some bad grain, Jack.

43

HUNTER: Jive, I don't want to see acid, much less taste it . . . It makes me think I'm the Jolly Green Giant . . . Ask Honey Man about acid.

RUBBER BAND: Yeah . . . He really got messed up on that stuff.

HUNTER: He once tied a bed sheet around his neck, thinkin' it was a cape.

RUBBER BAND: . . . and jumped . . .

HUNTER: . . . from the Watts Tower . . .

They all laugh.

RUBBER BAND: No lie . . .

HUNTER: He tried to fly . . .

RUBBER BAND: Hey, yeah. He got hung up thinking he was "Super Spook."

JIVE: "Super Spook?"

They all laugh.

HUNTER: Yeah. Yeah.

WEASEL *and* HONEY MAN *have been doing some head-to-head talking apart from the group.*

WEASEL: Get ourselves together and vote him out . . .

44

HONEY MAN: I told you you can't bring up no votin' jazz, Weasel.

JIVE: Votin'? (*Rises, moves toward* WEASEL.) Who's talking about votin'?

WEASEL (*backing away*): I'm talking private business with my man.

JIVE: Private what?

WEASEL: Private business. With him.

JIVE (*goes back to his desk and sits down*): Well, if you're talkin' about votin', you got to be talkin' about me; and if you're talkin' about me, you know it can't stay private too long, Weasel.

HONEY MAN: You got the wrong politician, Weasel.

JIVE: That's right, Weasel. There you go again with that conspiracy talk. You must think I'm some kind of a George Wallace trying to get in that bullshit White House. Wallace was dumb. I ain't dumb. I'm already king. There ain't no votin' in my kingdom. Only the king votes. I, me, I'm the king.

WEASEL (*thinks about this*): What do you mean, no votin', Man?

JIVE: 'Cause I said no votin'.

WEASEL: What kind of country you think this is, anyway?

JIVE: I don't think, I know. That's why I went out and got my own country.

HONEY MAN: Shit, you livin' in Jive's country now, Baby.

WEASEL: Oh, is that so, huh?

JIVE (*lecturing him*): That is so, HUH! And if you don't like it here, you better hope you got enough to live and eat on, 'cause outside this gig it is cold, cold, cold. And you know somethin' else, Weasel, I don't even want to talk about it any more. I got my own problems. All I know is that I started this organization. I got the government money. I got it integraded. I got it famous . . . I found Big Time, and if he sticks with me, he's goin' to find himself on top, a new leader, and we sure are in sor-ry need for . . . a . . . new . . . (JIVE *lets* HONEY MAN *finish the thought.*)

HONEY MAN: . . . LEADER, yeah.

RUBBER BAND: Big Time ain't sayin' it, Jack.

HUNTER: He ain't turned me on, yet.

WEASEL: Hell, no!

JIVE (*still lecturing*): He ain't suppose to turn you

on, *YET*. The last time somebody turned you nuts on, you almost burned down half the nation. Do you realize how hard it was for me to get this . . . group such a good reputation for bein' liberalized, huh? Do you realize that I was able to get the government's permission to invite a real live Grand Wizard from the Alabama Ku Klux Klan to come all the way up here and talk to you nuts on the Viet Nam situation? And what . . . WHAT does one of you idiots do? You slips the cat some acid!

RUBBER BAND: You bet your sweet red ass I slipped the cat some acid!!!

They all laugh, except JIVE.

JIVE (*goes after* RUBBER BAND): You better hope I don't get into any trouble over it, hear . . .

RUBBER BAND: What you gonna do about it, huh?

JIVE: I just got a telegram from them people today sayin' that they saw their boy on nationwide TV marching in some freedom parade someplace. All because of you. We'll probably get in trouble and be called Communist or CIA-financed or somethin' . . .

RUBBER BAND: Ah, why don't you just take care of some business?

ALL: Yeah, let's take care o' business.

47

JIVE: Honey Man, give me a count of these people here . . . (*Goes back to his desk, stands, waiting.*)

HONEY MAN (*moves into audience and up the aisle*): One . . . two . . . three . . .

WEASEL (*with disgust, watches* HONEY MAN *trying to count*): Honey Man, you suppose to be this cat's right-hand man, you can't even count . . . you dumb.

HONEY MAN (*turns on* WEASEL, *then rushes back on stage*): Weasel, every time I start to do somethin', you are always interfering, Man. I'm tired of you doin' that.

WEASEL: Hey, Man. Hell! Yeah, I'll interfere.

Intermixed argument, with HUNTER *and* RUBBER BAND *trying to break it up.*

JIVE (*moves in and breaks it up*): Shut up! Just shut up, Rubber Band . . . Weasel! . . . Now all you cats know the rules. I said all you cats know the rules . . .

ALL: Rules . . . Yeah . . .

They all come down into "formation" at front of stage, confronting the audience. JIVE *takes the center.*

48

JIVE (*addresses the audience, with his saccharine smile*): The game is "rules" . . .

ALL: Yeah.

JIVE: . . . and the rules are tough.

ALL: Yeah.

JIVE: Now these tough rules, Ladies and Gentlemen, are designed to establish peace . . . and dignity.

HONEY MAN: Yeah.

JIVE: Breaking the rules is breaking the peace and the dignity. Peace and dignity will not be broken . . .

ALL: Not tonight.

JIVE: We know where you all are at . . . and that rides pretty high . . . so if any of you are here to be breaking the rules . . .

ALL: Yeah!

JIVE: . . . or the peace . . .

ALL: Yeah!

JIVE: . . . or the dignity . . .

ALL: Yeah!

JIVE (*forgetting himself, he raises his fist*): I'll take my big fist and come down there and . . .

49

ALL (*they try to restrain* JIVE): Hey, Jive. Hey! Hey! Sucker! Don't do that, Man!

WEASEL (*spots someone in audience*): Hey, Man. That guy out there is chewin' gum!

They all see him and start protesting.

JIVE (*all sweetness again*): Order. Order. Order! Order! . . . Ah . . . Ladies and Gentlemen . . . cigarette smoking and gum chewing is out. We can't have any bad habits displayed while Big Time addresses you. Now the man is a little late gettin' here, so I'm goin' to take this time to bring you people up to date on what's been happening with BAD.

HUNTER: Run it on down, Man.

WEASEL: Yeah.

JIVE (*sits at desk*): We're not goin' to waste any more time. We're goin' to go straight to the core of the problem . . . I'm goin' to talk to our . . . "Whitey" members about that last party . . .

ALL (*protesting*): Whitey? You oughta talk to *all* members! . . . Why?

JIVE: Because I am disturbed.

HUNTER: Disturbed about what?

JIVE: I'm disturbed at the way our "Whitey" membership in BAD has been *declining!*

ALL (*they consider that carefully*): That's cool!

JIVE: Now last week, Ladies and Gentlemen, last week we had seventeen dropouts.

WEASEL: Right!

JIVE: That's a major blacklash . . . A major "*Whitey*" backlash.

ALL: Right!

JIVE: Now you people must understand that in the beginning BAD was made up of some of the really meanest cats I know . . .

ALL: Right. Yeah.

JIVE: We used to be out in them streets . . .

HONEY MAN (*throws a big punch*): . . . in them back alleys . . .

HUNTER (*demonstrates*): . . . with lead pipes . . .

RUBBER BAND (*demonstrates*): . . . knockin' down cops . . .

HONEY MAN (*smiling*): . . . and burnin' up things . . .

JIVE: . . . That's right. And all of a sudden these

51

same beautiful cats here got caught up in the
. . . this . . .

HONEY MAN (*supplying the right words*): This co-existence type thing . . .

JIVE: Yeah . . . I mean you people just got to . . . You people just got to understand that these same cats here still get a big kick out of beating white people up and . . .

ALL (*protesting, trying to cool* JIVE): Hey . . . Hey . . . What you sayin', huh? What you trying to say? . . . You must be losin' yo' mind . . .

JIVE: All I'm trying to say, Ladies and Gentlemen, all I'm trying to say is that if this backlash dropout stuff continues, these cats are goin' to be back out in them alleys with them lead pipes beating your . . .

ALL: Hey! Hey! What you doin'? Be cool!! Hey!

RUBBER BAND: Are you losin' your mind? Why you blame everything on Brothers, anyway? Huh, Man?

JIVE: I don't blame everything on Brothers. I got it right down here in black and white, and I know who caused that riot . . .

They all dive for desk, and start digging, looking for the "black and white."

ALL: Where, Man? . . . Where? . . . Where, Man?

JIVE: GET OFF OF MY DESK! GET OFF OF MY DESK! (*All pull back.*) THAT'S A NO-NO. Now the direct cause, as far as I can see, of what happened at that last party, (*He checks them over.*) was our review board.

ALL (*they consider that carefully*): That's right. Uh huh!

JIVE: Now, our review board, our review board went ahead, and in order to bring both sides together more, decided to name that last party "Whitey, Surprise your Black Brothers and Sisters with a Gift."

WEASEL: Yeah.

RUBBER BAND: That's right.

JIVE: Now that was the second time they gave that name to a monthly party.

HUNTER: Second time . . .

JIVE: And that was the second time they gave all forty-three black Brothers and Sisters fried chicken, the dirty Motherf . . .

ALL (*jumping in, protesting*): Hey . . . what you sayin'? You losin' your mind, Sucker?

JIVE: AW . . . SHUT UP! (*He rises from desk.*) All right! Hunter's got the good money plate.

53

HUNTER: Right here!

JIVE: And you people ought to know the High Rule on this now . . . Big Time don't answer no questions unless that plate is tapped with scratch.

ALL: Yeah.

JIVE: You got to tap that plate before he answers your question.

ALL: Yeah!

JIVE: This is the High Rule Number One.

ALL: Yeah!

JIVE: Number One: Big Time rules . . .

ALL: Yeah!

JIVE: The Rule of Plate Tappin'.

ALL: Yeah!

JIVE: So for God's sake, please don't go agitating the man unless you're ready to tap that plate.

ALL: Yeah!

JIVE: Honey Man, show these nice people here how to make the plate scene, Brother. (*He sits back down.*)

HUNTER: Tap the plate, Honey Man.

They all close in on HONEY MAN, *who begins searching his pockets for some change.*

WEASEL: Hey, tap the plate, Honey Man. Tap the plate. Hey, Honey Man.

HUNTER: Honey Man, show them how to *tap* the plate.

HONEY MAN (*quite embarrassed*): Just be cool, now, be cool . . . (*Finding no change in his pocket, he tries to spot a "sucker" in the audience. He sees* WHITEY.) Hunter, that gentleman over there (*He points him out.*) . . . the one behind the lady . . . the one in the grey . . . Hunter, have *him* tap the plate.

HUNTER (*spots the man*): This one? . . . (*They nod. To* WHITEY.) Sir, would you mind standing up, please? (*They all smile.*)

WHITEY (*standing nervously. Mumbles*): Well, uh, what do I do? . . .

HUNTER: We want you to tap the plate.

ALL (*as* WHITEY *reaches for change*): That's it . . . go right ahead . . . tap that plate . . . don't be nervous . . . show us how you do it . . . it's just practice, mister . . .

WHITEY *drops coin in plate.*

55

HUNTER (*immediately*): *Now sit down!* (WHITEY *obeys.* HUNTER *starts back to the stage. All ad lib "thank yous" and start to move back to* JIVE. HUNTER *remains at the front of the stage, checking the coin. Finding it's just a dime, he peers out angrily at* WHITEY *and mouths,*) *"You dirty Motherfucker!"* (*To* JIVE.) JIVE . . . A THIN DIME! (*To* WHITEY.) *You don't bring me no damn dime, Mister!*

ALL (*starting to go after* WHITEY): WHAT! . . . Hey, Man . . . What you doin'?

JIVE (*rises; moves between them to front of stage. In the process, he sneaks the dime into his pocket*): Order! Order! Where is he? (*They indicate.*) Look, you. Don't you ever come in here puttin' no stinkin' thin dimes in that plate. (*More sweetly.*) That goes for each and every one of you, too. Yeah, the minimum is two bits, Ladies and Gentlemen, to hear Big Time speak.

They all start to move back.

RUBBER BAND: I ain't ever seen no less.

HUNTER: I mean Big Time wouldn't like that.

JIVE: Right. The minimum is two bits per person, thank you. (*He returns to the desk.*)

WEASEL: Y'all better bring some quarters!

56

HUNTER (*checking the plate*): AH!!! OOO!!!

HONEY MAN: What's the matter, Hunter?

HUNTER: Jive done copped the dime!

ALL (*close in on* JIVE): Oh, NO!! Come on!!

WEASEL: Nigger stole the cat's dime, Man.

RUBBER BAND: You put that money right back in that plate, Sucker. No, you just put that money right back in that plate.

JIVE *is digging deep in his pocket.*

HUNTER: He didn't give us but a dime!

WEASEL: Give it back, Sucker.

RUBBER BAND: You must be losin' your mind, Baby!

WEASEL: Put that money in the plate, Man.

JIVE *finally gets dime into plate.*

JIVE (*points at* WHITEY): He made me forget what I was doing! (*With mock sincerity.*) I ain't gonna steal no stinkin' dime.

RUBBER BAND: Shit . . . Big Time see you pocketin' bread, you sure as hell forget what you doin'.

JIVE: What d' you mean, Baby?

RUBBER BAND: What you mean, "What I mean?"

57

JIVE: You heard me; What do you mean?

RUBBER BAND: Big Time will split your face so bad, you'll be picking your nose where your ears is, you pull that shit.

JIVE: Oh, I would?

WEASEL (*jumps right into his eardrum*): HELL YEAH YOU WOULD, MAN! You know you ain't got no business takin' no bread out of that plate, Jive . . . Hey, Man, you been callin' people niggers . . .

JIVE: You are niggers.

WEASEL: . . . You been threatening people, Jive . . . We gonna put you on the White List.

HONEY MAN: VOTE!

RUBBER BAND: Vote.

HUNTER: Vote! Let's Vote!

HONEY MAN: Vote!

WEASEL: We'll vote you outta here, Jive! We'll . . . It's about time we stood up together and got to votin'. Honey Man, we all got to vote some time, Brother. Vote! (WEASEL *is sure he is a winner*.)

HONEY MAN (*pauses, then moves behind* JIVE): Not me, Weasel . . . You know.

WEASEL: My Man The Hunter! Vote, Baby!

HUNTER (*evades him, goes to his man* JIVE): What fo', Sucker!

WEASEL: What do you mean, "what for"? Hey, Man. You told me you were voting for me.

HUNTER: Well, dig, Weasel. I got My *Own* Thing to do . . . You know. (*Smiles to house.*)

WEASEL: MY . . . MAIN . . . MAN . . . RUBBER . . . BAND! Tell 'em who *you* votin' for.

RUBBER BAND (*a long pause to consider this. Quietly*): *Me.*

WEASEL: Hey, Man. You told me you were votin' for me, Man. You told me you were votin' for *me,* Sucker.

RUBBER BAND: You too little to be a leader, Brother.

WEASEL (*comes right up under him*): You Uncle Tom.

RUBBER BAND: Huh? What you say, Man?

WEASEL: YOU UNCLE TOM!

RUBBER BAND: Aw naw, Sucker. I don't play that shit. Uh uh. I do not play it! Do you hear! I do not. (*He goes to blackboard, takes a piece of chalk, and draws a line on the floor.*) Do

59

you see that line? Do you see that line right there, Boy? Do you see that line?

WEASEL: Who you callin' "Boy?"

RUBBER BAND: YOU . . . Do you see that line right there, Boy? I dare you to cross that line. Don't cross that line. Do you understand that? Do not cross that . . . (*He decides to include* JIVE, *too.*) That goes for you too, high yella'.

HUNTER *and* HONEY MAN *clear the deck for action, whisking away the desk and chair and pushing the benches out of the way while they all shout "Oooooo! Oooooo! Ooooooooo!"*

HUNTER: I heard what he said.

JIVE (*getting up*): I'm gonna cross the line.

RUBBER BAND: Yeah. You sure are goin' to look funny without no feet, Jack.

JIVE: You see, you been ghetto-ized too long . . . I'll come over there and crack your kneecaps open.

RUBBER BAND (*putting his hand into his back pocket*): Uh huh. That's right. Come on. Come on, Man.

HONEY MAN *grabs* JIVE; HUNTER *grabs* HONEY MAN.

60

HONEY MAN: Watch out, Jive. He's got his street temper up, Man.

JIVE: Take your hand out-cha pocket.

RUBBER BAND: O.K., you're so brave, come on over here.

HUNTER: Jive, cool it.

JIVE (*not really trying to get loose*): It's a good thing you holding me back. You know, as bad as I am, I ain't gonna fool with no ghetto-ized spook.

HONEY MAN: Not while he can see you anyway, Man.

JIVE: Just look at him . . . He's hate infested . . . He's got all that hate just eatin' up and down inside his brain and chest . . .

HUNTER: Walkin' around lookin' crazeeeeeee!

JIVE: Now how do I know that behind them shades two insane lookin' eyeballs ain't sendin' a picture of me to his brain in blond hair and blue eyes.

ALL: You don't . . .

HONEY MAN: Really . . . he's vicious. He just don't give a damn no more.

JIVE: That's right. And a cat that don't give a

damn no more will chop through his nasty,
greasy lookin' Mammy to get to "Whitey."

HUNTER: Oh. Uh uh . . . Jive . . . I don't think
Rubber Band like you talking about his nasty,
greasy lookin' Mammy . . . And I don't
think Rubber Band sees how bad *Weasel* is
lookin' at him!

ALL: Ah ha! Uh huh! UH HUH! Uh huh! Weasel!
Uh huh!

HONEY MAN: Weasel ain't jivin'.

HUNTER: That's right.

RUBBER BAND: Shit.

JIVE: Look at Weasel . . .

HUNTER: . . . Weasel will straighten out your bow-
legs.

HONEY MAN: Yeah. You gotta watch them little
Brothers, Man.

JIVE: Weasel will jump up and cut you . . . he'll
run up and down your head with a lawn mower.

HONEY MAN: He is so bad he only gets high on
nerve gas.

HUNTER: He's so mean he'll wait for you . . .

JIVE: . . . knowin' that you gotta go to sleep one
of these days.

HONEY MAN: Weasel is an extremist!

JIVE: Mean, bad, blood-Brother extremists like Weasel like to keep to themselves.

Slowly but surely they are convincing WEASEL *that he's* BAD.

HUNTER: . . . like to live alone . . .

JIVE: . . . like to do a whole bunch of walkin' . . .

HONEY MAN: . . . He owns a white dog . . .

HUNTER: . . . wears Tyrone Power clothes . . . (WEASEL *spits at* RUBBER BAND, *who jumps back.*) Oh, Lordy!

RUBBER BAND: HEY, SUCKER!

JIVE: Ooooooo. And they like to spit a lot, too.

RUBBER BAND (*softening. To* WEASEL): You know I was just jivin', Brother. Come on and cross the line, Jack. Shit. Come on—cross the line, Brother. You know I was just jivin'. Come on, Brother.

WEASEL (*laughing about it now*): KNOW I'M BAD!

All laugh and enjoy it.

HUNTER (*he sees someone coming down the aisle. In awe*): Hey, here he comes, Baby! Big Time Buck White is here!

63

All scatter, getting into formation.

JIVE (*like a preacher welcoming the Lord*): Fill the mountains, Brothers . . .

ALL: Yeah.

JIVE: Fill the mountains with your cries of . . .

ALL: ANGER! ANGER! ANGER!

JIVE: Big Time Buck White, your serene teacher of good teaching thoughts is *here!*

ALL: Yeah! Yeahhhhhhhhhhhh!

BIG TIME BUCK WHITE *is on stage. They all applaud him.*

BIG TIME: Good evening and welcome to a meeting of B-A-D. I'm still reading in newspapers about Watts. What is what with Watts . . . There's a lot of people still talking about Watts. There's still a lot bein' shown on television, bein' read in newspapers and magazines! There's too much philosophizin' going on about Watts. There's so much bein' said *about* Watts, that the people who live *in* Watts are becoming confused . . . about what's what with Watts. It's complicated. And I never seen so many reasons for building a big bonfire . . .

HONEY MAN: Yeah.

64

BIG TIME (*emotional, but cool*): You know . . .
it sent me back . . . it sent me back to our
first day here. On our first day here they took
away everything we lived for . . . On the
first day they thought they squeezed us dry
. . . and the second day, that second day, they
got meaner . . . the second day they bit into
our lips with sticks . . . and it was on the
second day that we spit blood back at the
sucker's feet and told him WE HAVE AL-
WAYS BEEN . . .

ALL: Yeah.

BIG TIME: WE WILL ALWAYS BE!

ALL: Yeah!

BIG TIME: And it was on the second day that he
knew that we were stronger . . .

ALL: Yeah!

BIG TIME: And stronger!

ALL: Yeah!

BIG TIME: And stronger!!

ALL: Yeah!

BIG TIME: And stronger!!!

ALL: Yeah!

BIG TIME: And STRONGER!!!!

ALL: Yeah!

BIG TIME: And Big Time Buck White *is*.

ALL: Yeah!!!

BIG TIME: *Has always been.*

ALL: Yeah!

BIG TIME: *Will always be!*

ALL: Yeah!

BIG TIME: And that's what I'm here to talk about this evening. I'm here . . . to . . . uh . . . glory in my essence . . . The cymbals clash. The hungry men peel away the dust. The fruit is uncovered . . . new generations, Brothers. There is a hot burning spear . . .

ALL: Oh, yeah!

BIG TIME: It's a high torch!

ALL: Oh, yeah!

BIG TIME: . . . And it's finally marching through history! . . .

ALL: Oh, yeah!

BIG TIME: There is no time but *now!*

ALL: Oh, yeah.

66

BIG TIME: There is no place but *here!*

ALL: Yeah!

BIG TIME: AND I'M PROUD TO BE PART OF IT.

ALL: YEAH!

BIG TIME: . . . My name is Big Time Buck . . .

JIVE (*interrupting, gestures toward a tape recorder in the corner*): Get all that, Honey Man?

HONEY MAN: Huh?

JIVE: The tape, Baby.

> HONEY MAN *shakes his head.* JIVE, *disgusted, turns to* HUNTER.

Did you . . .

HUNTER: I *told* him to set it up; he knows his job.

BIG TIME: My name . . .

JIVE (*to* HUNTER): You mean that this man has been standing up here for five minutes talking his butt off and that tape recorder ain't on?

> HONEY MAN *runs to turn on the machine.*

All that stuff is gone? Why didn't you tell him to turn it on instead of standin' here talking to this nut?

HUNTER: I *did* tell him to turn it on.

JIVE: Why'd we let you in here?

HUNTER: I did tell him . . . and if he forgot, then *I'm shocked.*

HONEY MAN (*to* HUNTER): What you mean, shocked, Man?

BIG TIME: Jive. Jive! Jive, please, Man!

JIVE (*stares* HONEY MAN *down*): Oh, I'm sorry, Big Time.

WEASEL (*to* HONEY MAN): You big dummy.

JIVE (*to audience*): Ah . . . Ladies and Gentlemen, just tune right back in. And don't be afraid to feel ashamed of yourselves . . . (*Moves back to his position.*)

BIG TIME: My name is Big Time Buck White and I don't glory in someone else's country that someone else built up. I glory right c'here . . . right c'here . . . Now, why do I glory right c'here?

RUBBER BAND: Why not?

BIG TIME: All right, why not? Why not glory right c'here? We been right c'here four hundred years . . . We first came here four hundred years ago, as first-class passengers aboard a wet prison of death called "The African Disease"

68

. . . We didn't see Old Lady Liberty wavin' us
in, no we did not . . . But we saw a willow
on the bayou bow its head . . . in shame.
Welcome . . . Welcome . . . Welcome   to
the shores of freedom . . . by a smiling nut
deviate who made a deal with glistening black
muscles . . .

ALL: Yeah.

BIG TIME: . . . Promise me strong children . . .
to chop cotton off of conceited bushes that
stand free in the Alabama sun . . . and I'll
give you a rent-free swamp shack with wall-
to-wall dirt . . . I'll give you the privilege of
witnessing grinding childbirth screams shake
fear into night-owls. . . .

ALL: Yeah.

BIG TIME: *There* is the knowledge of life, Brothers
. . . These Brothers here have seen and known
that knowledge . . .

ALL: Oh, yeah!

BIG TIME: I said knowledge of life . . .

ALL: Yeah.

BIG TIME: Oh yeah!

ALL: Yeah!

BIG TIME: I mean knowledge of life, Brothers . . .

ALL: Oh, yeah.

BIG TIME: These hands, these hands have felt the knowledge . . . These hands have felt the warmth of life introduced to the exposure of invisible hate . . . and right then we felt a CHILL!

ALL: Yeah!

BIG TIME: WE FELT A CHILL!!

ALL: Yeah!!

BIG TIME: WE HAVE SEEN MORE LIFE SLIP DOWN . . . than stand up.

ALL: Yeah. Hmmmm. Yeah.

BIG TIME: Oh, yeah! . . . Yet somehow because there is a guiding spirit and the spirit is in my people . . . I sense the Almighty meanings . . . in the rhapsodies of nature . . .

ALL: Hmmm. Oh, yeah.

BIG TIME: And sung me a song.

ALL: Yeah.

BIG TIME: And dreamed . . .

WEASEL: Yeah.

BIG TIME: We dreamed to feel warm whippoorwill
sounds that cry distant and made birds . . .
OH YEAH . . . AND MADE BIRDS . . .

ALL: YEAH!

BIG TIME: . . . . AND   MADE   BIRDS
SCREEEEEEEEEEAAM!

ALL: Oh yeah!

BIG TIME: To the sky just to dream . . .

ALL: Yeah.

BIG TIME: To the sky just to dream. It made birds
scream to the sky just to sigh . . .

ALL: Yeah.

BIG TIME: It made birds scream . . .

ALL (*whooping it up*): Yeah . . . Yeah . . . too
much . . . too much . . . whoooeee . . .
whhoooeeeee . . . powerful . . . too much . . .

JIVE: How's it comin', Honey Man? Loud?

HONEY MAN (*as he goes over to check the recorder*):
Loud!

JIVE: Clear?

HONEY MAN: Clear!

JIVE: Strong?

71

HONEY MAN: Strong, too, Man . . . the tape just ate it up . . .

HUNTER: Ate it up?

HONEY MAN: Just blew the tubes right out, Baby . . .

JIVE: Ladies and gentleman, we're goin' to get a picture of BAD at its best to send to Washington, so bear with us for a moment, please. Rubber Band, take the picture.

WEASEL: It's my turn!

RUBBER BAND: Watch yourself, Sucker.

HUNTER: Jive, are you the boss?

WEASEL *and* RUBBER BAND *are still hollering.*

JIVE: Of course I'm the boss.

HUNTER: Well, control these niggers.

JIVE: Get into position.

Grouping, they stand tensely.

HUNTER: Fold your arms.

RUBBER BAND: Smile. (*They smile. The picture taken,* RUBBER BAND *hands camera back to* HONEY MAN.)

72

JIVE: Ladies and Gentlemen, the meeting is now back on. Big Time Buck White is now open for questions . . . Question time . . .

During the following improvisational question-and-answer period, which was compiled from several performances during the New York run, there are twelve questioners: four plants and eight genuine questioners. QUESTIONER #3 *is* WHITEY, *an actor and the only obvious plant.* [P = Plant; G = Genuine questioner.]

QUESTIONER #1-P (*white girl*): Over here.

HUNTER: Tap the plate. (*He rushes down.*)

QUESTIONER #1: Mister Buck White, do you like white people?

HUNTER: Did she say what I thought she said?

ALL: WHAT? WHAT THE HELL DID SHE SAY? WHAT?

JIVE: Order! Order . . . Now the lady asked Big Time Buck White a question . . . Big Time Buck White will answer the question.

BIG TIME (*pauses, decides it does not deserve an answer*): *Next* question.

WEASEL: See? You can't trust none of them Whiteys. They all a bunch of Birchers.

RUBBER BAND: That's O.K., Brother, cause I *love* to hate.

JIVE: Could we have some more questions?

RUBBER BAND: Dig hatin', Brother.

WEASEL: Dig hate . . . Dig hate.

JIVE: I would like to tell you people a little about the history of Big Time Buck White . . .

BIG TIME: Hey, Jive . . . you got some nice people out there tonight. Yes, you have.

JIVE: Some beauts!

BIG TIME: Let's get back to the questions.

QUESTIONER #2-P (*white man*): Mister Big Buck, does BAD represent itself as being a force in *favor* of Law or *against* it?

BIG TIME: Animals don't have laws, birds don't have laws, bees don't, the only thing in this universe that has laws is man, man he's got his laws. He created laws because man knew that man was a beast. He chewed up maggot-filled dogs and sucked the venom-juice out of reindeer eyeballs. I'm talkin', I'm talkin', I'm talkin' about history, history, fifty thousand years ago, and it seems like today, because today man is filled with useless law. For this is a Great Society

74

that's being born here, free thinkers go to jail, simple souls go to heaven, 'cause laws are obeyed and Lord knows a Whitey obeys laws. He drinks his water from pure white fountains, excremates that good food he eats in lily-white toilets, he even walks the white sidewalks and tells us that Law is a thing he created that teaches him against death. But the walkin' mud of Mississippi is staining those shoes with mud, there's another thing happenin', there's a beauty here that knows before it's told what is right and what is wrong, it knows that your life is the most precious thing you'll ever have and it's your life and your death, and it knows your death is just like what Ray Charles says, when you're dead you die, yes, you die. So crush those timeless laws and useless laws and let man create his own universal form so that men can stand up straight and walk their own little dark areas in life.

JIVE (*cutting in*): O.K. No more laws. Now, next question . . .

RUBBER BAND: Hey Man, the cat's talkin' about Mississippi, Man.

JIVE: Well I want to go somewhere else.

RUBBER BAND: There ain't nothing wrong with talking about a live, uptight, white Baptist, black-hating Mississippi law, you mahogany Eskimo.

JIVE: Shut up, you don't understand nothing, dummy.

HUNTER: Godammit, Jive.

JIVE: I'll close this meeting.

HUNTER: Don't tell a man he don't understand nothin'.

RUBBER BAND: That's right, Man.

JIVE: Ladies and Gentlemen the meeting is now closed. Goodnight.

ALL: Oh no . . . don't do that . . . Hey, Jive . . .

JIVE: What d'ya think you're doin', then?

BIG TIME (*quietly*): Do we have to show all these people how long we've been ostracized?

WEASEL: OSTRA . . . (*To* HONEY MAN.) What does he mean by "ostracized?"

JIVE: He means stop playing the part of—uh—John Wayne, you dummy.

WEASEL: John Wayne?

JIVE: That's right, John Wayne.

RUBBER BAND: I ain't no John Wayne, Sucker. What you talkin' about?

BIG TIME: I'm saying that as black men you can do one of two things. Now I don't think I have to say anything more about that.

WEASEL: Good. That's what he says at you Rubber Band. You gotta go around wearing those tight pants like some kind of peacock. . . . You got to prove to the whole world that you some kind of a super stud.

RUBBER BAND (*thinks about this*): I *am* Super Stud.

JIVE: Can we have some more questions?

WEASEL: Hey, Jive, nobody goes around callin' me no ostracized.

JIVE: Oh, shut up.

HUNTER (*spying a hand up, heads for audience*): Tap the plate. (*Questioner taps the plate.*)

QUESTIONER #3, WHITEY: Mister Buck White . . .

HUNTER (*checking the plate*): Mister, shut up . . .

WEASEL: Let's see that plate.

HUNTER (*shows plate to the Organizers*): He did it again. (*To the man in the audience.*) Mister, you owe me four hundred years' back wages! And Sucker, you goin' to pay me my money tonight! (*He starts out to get* WHITEY.)

77

ALL: Hunter, Hunter, go get him, get him, hey, Hunter, get him!

JIVE (*grabs* HUNTER): Come on back here, you. Are you out of your dumb, insipid, moronic little mind? You know we don't go beatin' up people anymore, and you know somethin', you are embarrassing me.

HUNTER: You ought to be.

BIG TIME (*quietly*): It's a shame that throughout history, man, in order to take the next step forward, he has always had to contend with power marches of mice.

HUNTER (*indignant*): *Mice?*

BIG TIME (*simply*): Mice. How many times has this quest for power destroyed the whole process of creativity? That's why a Hitler will make it and a Martin Luther King will get killed.

WEASEL: What you tryin' to say?

HUNTER (*his composure recovered, he speaks to* WHITEY): Tap this plate.

WEASEL: Hey, Jive, I'm bringing up another complaint, Man! Nobody goes around callin' me no "mice."

JIVE: Get back there, Weasel.

WEASEL *moves back into place.*

78

HUNTER: Tap the plate.

WHITEY (*ignores* HUNTER): Mister Buck White. How complex . . .

JIVE (*politely*): Oh, Sir, everytime you ask Big Time a question, you gotta tap that plate.

RUBBER BAND: Yeah, tap that plate, Mister.

WHITEY (*reluctantly drops a quarter in the plate*): How complex is the black and white situation back there in Watts?

HUNTER: *Sit down!* (HONEY MAN *chuckles. To* HONEY MAN.) It ain't funny.

BIG TIME: You see, the black situation in Watts is like the black situation in Harlem and in both cases it is not so much that the black man recognizes that the black man is an inferior man because the black man happens to be a black man. In both cases, it is more that the white man recognizes that the black man recognizes that the black man is an inferior man because he is a black man. Now all of a sudden the white man has gotten busy, and he's trying to tell the black man that he ain't got no reason trying to stay inferior. Well, no matter what happens to that black man, that black man can't turn white. Now that means that long as the white man is busy trying to tell the black man that the black man shouldn't stay inferior, that black man will never believe the white man wants the black man to be anything but inferior.

RUBBER BAND: Sure is complex, ain't it.

HONEY MAN: Worse than that, Rubber Band, worse than that, really.

JIVE waits for another question. He points out another questioner.

HUNTER: Tap the plate.

QUESTIONER #4-P (*white teenage boy*): Mister Buck White, when your friend here said this man owes you four hundred years in back wages, you know and I know that that is a lot of bull, because don't give me any of this original sin bit . . . that because I'm white, I owe you four hundred years' back pay . . . I . . .

BIG TIME (*cutting in*): You just listen to me one second here, please. I'm not at your job, kicking the spade out of your hand, you know.

QUESTIONER #4: Now look . . . I'm about seventeen years old, so how can you tell me that I owe you four hundred years of back wages? Say I was just born, now I might have inherited this situation, but don't go blaming me for the other three hundred eighty-three years of it.

BIG TIME: That's a good point, that's a real good point. Now, I wouldn't blame you for nothin' if you were trying to pose as a black man livin' in a black ghetto. But see, you are guilty. It doesn't make any difference whether you feel guilty, it doesn't make any difference whether you individually have castrated the black people or denied them any rights. If you're a white man and you enjoy the fruits of a nation that the black man has essentially built for nothin', you are dead.

JIVE: More questions? (*Sees a hand.*) You, sir.

HUNTER: Tap the plate. (HUNTER *sees it is a black man.*) It's a Brother!

RUBBER BAND (*looks over the audience*): Look at the Sister down there with the Brother . . . Shiiiit, Brothers gonna take over Manhattan Island.

WEASEL: Give it soul, Brother.

RUBBER BAND: Tight.

QUESTIONER #5-P (*black man*): You mentioned a few minutes ago about the black man taking away from the whites. You know, the black

81

man, white man thing . . . Could you re-
peat that a minute . . .

JIVE: Oh, no. That's a Brother all right you dumb
Mother . . .

ALL (*shouting at* JIVE): Hey, Jive . . . Hey . . .
what you doin'? . . .

BIG TIME (*quietly restoring order*): Hey, hey, hey
. . . What I'm tryin' to say is there are two
sides to that. And one of those sides is not
content unless they destroy beauty. They can't
look at beauty, they examine it, they got to
own it, they got to control it, they got to be
the father of it. They treat people like they're
children. Like a child that you oppress and
criticize until you get to the point where you've
done it too much and then you feel guilty
about the whole mess, so you buy the little
kiddy some toys to play with to make him
happy. Now you spend millions of dollars trying to make that little kiddy happy. Well, when
that little kiddy who is angry as a kid grows
up into a *man* who is angry, well then you
really in trouble. And if that anger persists
and if that black man understands he don't
have to stay, that he can leave, and when he
leaves he can take everything with him that
he owns, then you better hope that what he

82

owns ain't that house y'all been livin' in so comfortably all these years. What I'm trying to say is that guilt is the feelin' that you get from being a bully, after you've stepped on somebody. Next question.

JIVE: Next question.

HUNTER: Tap the . . . (*Sees it's* WHITEY *again.*) That same sucker! (HUNTER *looks at* BIG TIME, *who pacifies him with a stern glance. Meekly.*) Sorry, Big Time.

WHITEY: I'm not entirely sure, sir, but you said that a black man could go one of two ways, and I can see a situation today where a lot of white people are afraid that you people won't stop if you get the power that you want . . . that you'll go on and try and dominate everything. Now . . .

HONEY MAN (*breaking in*): DOMINATE! Hey, what the hell are you talkin' about, dominate?

ALL: Yeah . . . what you mean dominate?

WEASEL: Wait a minute, wait a minute. I want to answer this sucker. I'm gonna answer you hard.

BIG TIME (*contemplates a moment*): All right, Weasel, answer the man.

83

JIVE (*protesting*): Weasel can't answer the man. He's an idiot.

HONEY MAN *and* WEASEL *chuckle at* WEASEL'S *victory over* JIVE.

You better answer him right, you little black sambo.

ALL: Hey . . . don't call him that . . . who you think you are . . . sambo . . .

WEASEL (*moves to center. His big moment. He pauses, confused*): What was that question again?

ALL: Dominate, dominate, DOMINATE!

WEASEL (*to* WHITEY): Dominate? Don't you ever learn to talk . . . you're the one who's trying to dominate.

ALL: Yeah . . . that's right . . . yes, sir . . .

BIG TIME (*to* WHITEY): It don't seem like the Brothers liked the way you phrased your question. Could you rephrase it?

WHITEY: I don't feel that I was fully understood. Now, Mister Weasel . . .

Audience laughs.

JIVE (*to* WHITEY, *indicating* WEASEL): He ain't laughin'.

BIG TIME (*aside*): Weasel, I told you to take that African name yesterday.

WHITEY: Uh . . . Sir? If one goes back to the Civil War, when the North beat the South, and Lincoln allowed the slaves their freedom, and . . .

JIVE (*cutting him off*): Lincoln ALLOWED the slaves their freedom . . . Allowed, right? . . . Did you hear that "allowed?" . . . I want to . . . Damn, it makes me mad, you just think you know so much, don't you, boy? You come in here and you tell *me*, me being black, mind you, that I am allowed something. It doesn't matter if I already own it, hell no. I am black so I am *allowed* something back that was mine to begin with in the first place.

WHITEY: You don't understand . . .

JIVE: Well I understand.

WEASEL: It ain't your country anyway.

WHITEY: Well, I know that.

WEASEL: Who owns it then, who owns it?

WHITEY: Well, it belongs to . . .

WEASEL *and* RUBBER BAND: Who owns it?

WHITEY: Well, it's just that . . .

ALL (*pick up the chant*): Who owns it?

WHITEY: Well, I . . .

ALL: *Who owns it?*

WHITEY (*gives in*): You do.

WEASEL: Damn right I do. Don't come here telling me what to do with my country . . .

JIVE (*seeing cigarette smoke in the audience*): Hey, put that cigarette out. Who's smoking? Put it out. (*All help* JIVE *restore order to the meeting.*) Order. This happens to be the most undisciplined crowd to be here yet.

HONEY MAN (*right on* JIVE'S *heels*): This is the most undisciplined-est yet.

JIVE: Now, discipline and control is a very high solemn rule here. Without discipline and control . . . you didn't put the cigarette out, buster; the meeting is closed. I mean closed.

ALL (*protesting*): What's wrong with you . . . Hey wait a minute, Man . . . Don't close the meetin' . . . fine those suckers . . . we need the money . . . Hey, Jive . . . we ain't got no bread . . . come on, Man. . . .

JIVE: I am fining each of you fifty cents apiece, you bunch of uncouth . . .

ALL: That's right . . . tap the plate . . . house rules . . . fine 'em . . . get the plate. . . .

JIVE: Get all of 'em and get fifty cents out of each and every one of them and if they don't like it, kick them out. Start from over here, Honey Man . . . (HONEY MAN *starts toward audience with the plate.*)

BIG TIME: Honey Man. (*Motions him to return to the stage.*)

JIVE: What?

BIG TIME: Honey Man . . . the plate.

JIVE (*turns around to talk with* BIG TIME): What . . . what you doin'? . . . (*He and* BIG TIME *argue quietly.* JIVE *loses and returns to his place.*)

BIG TIME: Honey Man, put down the plate. (HONEY MAN *puts it on the desk.*) You Brothers don't seem to care how we act in front of the people. If you don't care how you act in front of the people, maybe you wouldn't care about calling a meeting right now.

ALL: Oh no, not a meeting . . . Hey, wait . . .

HUNTER: All we do is meet, meet, meet.

RUBBER BAND: Hey, Weasel, what you doin' with

the money in the plate? Put the money back
in the plate . . .

BIG TIME: You Brothers gonna have to understand
that this Organization just didn't happen by itself, a Brother worked hard to pull it together.
He organized the thing himself. He went out
on the street, he went out in the alleys, he
selected you Brothers to help him to do the
things that have to be done in any organization
this BAD. This Brother has brought dissimilar
elements together under one roof, so that when
you get ready to move, you can move together.
And the man's name is Jive.

HUNTER: We know that.

BIG TIME: I think the Brother should get some sup-
port from you. The man works into the wee
hours of the morning for your . . .

WEASEL: Damn it, Big Time, we all know that!
We all know that, Man. I got something I'm
going to say.

RUBBER BAND (*angry at* WEASEL *for interrupting*
BIG TIME): You better move back, Sucker
. . . Get back or I'll bite into your head,
Sucker. . . .

WEASEL: I got something I want to say, Brother.
Hey, Man. Hey . . .

88

RUBBER BAND: You are taxing my patience, Brother!

WEASEL: But . . . But . . . I got something . . .

RUBBER BAND (*moves* WEASEL, *step by step, into a chair*): Weasel, Weasel, Weasel . . . in your seat, don't you move once more, 'cause if you do, I'm going to take my hand, you see my hand, Weasel, and I am going to stick it down your throat and I am going to rip out your rectum.

WEASEL *is transfixed in sheer terror by* RUBBER BAND's *hand, inches from his face.* WEASEL *shuts up.* RUBBER BAND, *knowing he has won, relaxes, straightens up, and returns to his position. All, except* WEASEL, *who remains on the bench, return to their positions.*

BIG TIME: I don't know what's wrong with you Brothers today, I thought. . . .

JIVE: We had a party last night.

BIG TIME: I don't care about a party last night, this is not a party tonight, we're not having a party tonight. When I call a meeting I thought we had a meeting right then and there. I don't call meetings just to listen to the sound of my voice. I call them when I think you Brothers need them.

ALL (*agreeing*): You right, you're absolutely right . . . that's right . . .

BIG TIME: Weasel, I haven't heard your sweet voice, Brother.

WEASEL: Shit.

BIG TIME: O.K. Jive, I quit.

ALL (*alternately screaming at* WEASEL *for irritating* BIG TIME *and pleading with* BIG TIME): Goddamit Weasel . . . cut that out . . . no you don't . . . stop that . . . ah, you can't quit, Big Time . . . Oh, come on . . . Hey, Big Time, please don't quit . . . You can't quit, Big Time . . . Please, Big Time . . . don't quit. If Big Time quits . . .

JIVE (*trying to restore order*): Inspection time, and I mean inspection time, now! (*All move into position.*) Now, Ladies and Gentlemen, let's try if we can . . . let's all of us try if we can . . . to reach some kind of inner peace and tranquillity. Inner peace and tranquillity. Ladies and Gentlemen . . .

HONEY MAN (*in a loud whisper*): Hey, Jive, Jive, Jive . . .

JIVE: I'm talkin' to these people, will you just mind your . . .

HONEY MAN: Will you please just consider the situation, really. All this confusion and bickering and turmoil that's going on here, this is an appropriate time to seek out inner peace and tranquillity . . .

JIVE *stares* HONEY MAN *into silence.*

JIVE: Inner peace and tranquillity, Ladies and Gentlemen, think inner peace and tranquillity, so as Big Time's words can get purity from all of you. So let's go on giving him inner peace and tranquillity to feed on . . . (*A long pause. All close their eyes and search for that inner peace and tranquillity.*) Brothers, inner peace and tranquillity has cleared the air. (*All applaud and cheer.*)

HONEY MAN: A little peace will do it every time. (*He chuckles at his pun.*)

JIVE: More questions please, raise your hands.

HUNTER (*spots a hand up*): Tap the plate.

BIG TIME: *Free!*

ALL: Free? . . . Free? . . . Why free?

JIVE: Free Time, Ladies and Gentlemen . . . Free Time. Ladies and Gentlemen, for the next ten

minutes Big Time Buck White will answer any
questions that anyone has to ask, absolutely
freeee . . . Anything you want to ask the
man . . . You will no longer be inhibited by
the passing of the plate, just raise your hands.
(*Spots a hand up.*) All right, you, lady, next.

QUESTIONER #6-G (*white girl*): I don't understand,
what do you want, is it power or do you just
want to be equal, I just don't understand what
is going on. Explain it to me, I don't really
get it.

BIG TIME: You see, if you understand what our
Brothers mean . . .

JIVE (*with a hungry leer*): I'll make you understand what it's all about.

BIG TIME (*patiently*): If you understand what the
Brothers are talkin' about when they call the
white man a devil, little bitch, you'll understand that any man who wants to emulate the
devil or be equal to the devil is a fool. The
white man's values are much different from
the black man's. The white man glorifies violence. He's got a strange obsession with war
toys. When you talk about the glory of Rome,
we are talking about Rome's military strength;
when we talk about the glory that was England's, we are talking about England's control

of the high seas. We're talking about violence.
Why should a black man align himself with
that? We're not concerned with being equal,
we're not even concerned with hating white
people. We ain't got the time to hate white
people, we got too much to do ourselves. We
don't want to be equal. What we want, we'll
get, 'cause we have the power that's inherent
in us.

JIVE: More questions . . . Free questions . . .
come on . . . You, sir.

QUESTIONER #7-G (*white man*): I don't know what
you mean when you talk about violence. Are
you going to get busy and do something about
it or are you just going to sit around and talk
to a bunch of white people and be . . . irrelevant. I think that is the real question.

JIVE: I don't think it is the real question, I think
it's *your* question.

QUESTIONER #7: Well, *I* think it's the real question.

BIG TIME: If we're going to do something about the
white man's violence?

QUESTIONER #7: Yeah, what you gonna do about
the white man's violence?

93

BIG TIME: Well, what's happening is that the police department doesn't protect the black man, and so the black man is, to some extent, having to arm himself to protect himself. You know if you are a black man and you go down, you can't call upon the United States Army. Did you ever hear a black man say "Our Army?" Did you ever hear a black man say "Our President?" No. Now, what are we going to do about the violence? You know, we have a power ourselves. We don't have no big machines, we don't have no big control of the communications network, we don't have an army, we don't have a police force, and we don't even have much money, but I'm here to tell you that the black people *unified* have the power, the capability of *thinning out* this nation . . . You know, you can still get two books of matches for one penny in some places. (*He lets this sink in.*) . . . This is a system that I am for, the liberation of the black man on his own terms and I don't care how that happens. I think this revolution has to be a very cunning, witty, creative thing. What was infected yesterday, may not be infected today. So that you know what I was yesterday, I may not be tomorrow. You may have to do what is necessary to free the black man. If it means an all-out confrontation, that's what it means, but I hope it doesn't. . . .

JIVE: More questions please.

BIG TIME (*has an afterthought*): A system that won't allow a man to live as a man can't stop a man from dying as a man. One meaning of Black Power is that black people are men, and a man is just going to take so much. Malcolm said that if you were the man that you think you are, you'd figure out what you'd do and then you know what he'd do only he'd do more.

RUBBER BAND: That's right.

JIVE: O.K. now, more questions, Ladies and Gentlemen. Do I see another question? . . . You, there, Sister.

QUESTIONER #8-G *is a sophisticated-looking black woman in her late twenties.*

WEASEL: Ooooweee, check that out!

RUBBER BAND: With a Natural, too!

BIG TIME: Let's let the Sister talk.

QUESTIONER #8: What do you think of black women who still wear processed hair, like washed-out white women, I mean, after all that the white man has done to us for the last four hundred years, how can they have any pride in their blackness and keep tryin' to be white? Aren't they betraying everything that being black stands for?

BIG TIME: Easy now, Sister, easy . . . we got to have compassion for all black people. We all been oppressed for the last four hundred years, and underneath that oppression we got to realize we're all Brothers and Sisters. You must have gone through a lot before you could be the way you are—now, don't be so hard on your Sisters who haven't gone through all the changes yet. They're still Sisters and they'll be with us in good time. After all, like Rap says, better a natural man with processed hair than a processed man with natural hair.

RUBBER BAND: Tell it like it is, Big Time!

QUESTIONER #8: I can dig it.

JIVE: Next question, please.

QUESTIONER #9-G (*white man*): Do you allow for room in your revolution for white people or do you believe that we could never be part of you and you never part of us?

BIG TIME: Well see, Black Power is a kind of island where black people have to get away from that jazz that you've been laying on them for so many years. So that they have the time, and they have the space, and they have the opportunity and the environment to understand that's what they are: dignified, powerful, beautiful, black people. That they're dignified beings, see? Now we have to do our own thing in our own way. Now if a white person is interested in helping us directly, we don't need no help from whites. I don't think the Brothers need any help in Harlem. What you *can* do is after you leave this meeting you can go on home, and after you get home, you clean up your own marvelous mind, and then you clean up your father's mind, and your mother's mind, and after you get through with that you clean up your cousin's mind and then your neighbors' minds, and your brother's and sister's minds, and the community's minds, and I mean that's a lifetime occupation. If you did that, then you ain't gonna have time for no Harlem or Watts.

JIVE: Another question . . . Must be one intelligent, curious person down there . . . You, lady.

QUESTIONER #10-G (*white woman*): What do you think is the meaning of recent proposals by such people as Richard Nixon and other leaders concerning something called Black Capitalism?

97

BIG TIME: That's a variation, that's another label for green power. Jive here sometimes gets off a little too much in that bag of green power . . . I ask all of you to remember what happened to Confederate money.

JIVE: They can't do that to my money if it's in the Swiss banks. . . . More questions, Ladies and Gentlemen, you, sir, stand up please, stand up please. Please stand up, you gotta stand up cause they can't hear you in the rear.

QUESTIONER #4 (*white boy*): You talk about terms, just what are your terms?

BIG TIME: Will you get off my back? You aren't guilty, O.K.? White people along with black people should work for the liberation of the black man, they should work toward the black man achieving some kind of say in his destiny, the things that control his life, because the white man has been continually giving us his version of freedom since the Emancipation Proclamation, but what a white man means when he says freedom usually ain't the same thing that a black man means when he says freedom, 'cause as long as you controlling somebody, how can you call it freedom?

QUESTIONER #4: You're condemning the white

man for the same thing that you're doing right
now. Using generalities and not being specific.

BIG TIME: Well then, ask me somethin' specific.

QUESTIONER #4: Well, I asked . . . Well, where's
it all going to end? You're doing the same
thing as you've been accusing us of doing.
You're just throwing out hate like heaped-up
garbage.

JIVE (*sweetly*): Do *I* look like I hate you?

QUESTIONER #4: Often the most powerful form of
hate is a smile.

JIVE: HA, HA, HA.

BIG TIME: Here's a white man that's been talking
to a black man. Look, Man, if you got something to say, I gave you an opportunity to say
it. All right? It's my turn now. O.K.?

QUESTIONER #4: O.K.

BIG TIME: Why don't you all be quiet now.

JIVE: That's right, you remember that.

BIG TIME: Now, that's the thing, you accuse us of
hating, we ain't got the time to hate. We ain't
even concerned with you. That's the whole
thing, you feel left out and . . . and you
know, the white man *would* pick up a label
like hate. Now there's a label. White man's

got that label thing down, got to give him credit for that. He'll label himself out of two continents. He labeled himself into the Americas. Here he is with his tradition, with his lily-white god, with his way of living, with his mores, with his culture, and his laws, and his kind of regulation; and merely because there are people across the ocean who live differently, that worship different gods, that have different traditions and he thinks he can go over there from this country to that country, ravish the land, rape the women, murder off the good men, if you do it under the disguise of the label "settler." A settler ain't nothin' but a land grabber. A settler ain't nothin' but a murderer, and if you term these people, because they don't live the same way as you do and they don't worship your god, if you term them savages, that means that you could do with them whatever you want. That's where a label can kill you. A label can really kill you. You know white people talking about improving the black man's condition, like getting the black man to join a country club, and the black man talking about improving his condition; it's not the same. I'm trying to say, you want me to do it your way and I want to do it my way. When you say something and I say something, they don't mean the same thing.

JIVE: More questions, Ladies and Gentlemen . . . you, lady . . .

QUESTIONER #11-G (*white woman*): That sign behind you says WIPE OUT WHITE WOMEN. What do you mean by that?

JIVE: What do you think we mean? Stand up.

BIG TIME: I want to know where that question came from . . . (*He spots her.*) Do you know what a bleaching cream is?

QUESTIONER #11: Excuse me?

BIG TIME: Do you know what a bleaching cream is?

QUESTIONER #11: Yes.

BIG TIME: Hey, I can't see her out there.

JIVE (*assuring him*): She's white, she's white.

BIG TIME: I see silhouettes mostly . . . Now, do you know what a do-rag is?

QUESTIONER #11: No.

BIG TIME: Why didn't you ask me about the do-rag?

QUESTIONER #11: Because I'm not a do-rag, I'm a white woman.

BIG TIME: Don't you know what "wipe out" means? . . . I mean, what is the question about?

101

QUESTIONER #11: Well, then I'll ask you, what do you mean by wipe out? I mean, it could mean a lot of things.

JIVE (*smiling*): We really hate to tell you.

QUESTIONER #11: Well, then, how about this do-rag. What's a do-rag?

BIG TIME: Maybe it's none of your business.

JIVE: More questions . . . (*Recognizes a black questioner and urges him on.*) Relax, Brother, you're free here . . . Don't worry about a thing . . .

QUESTIONER #12 (*black man*): I think Mr. Nixon's term Black Capitalism is similar to White Capitalism where it's only been working for a few people. I mean, where it's only going to be good for those black people who have money and give them more. But it's not going to do anything for the mass of black people . . .

BIG TIME (*agreeing*): That's right, it's just a token gesture, you know white people control the communication media so you sure are gonna hear about only what those white controllers want you to hear, especially from a President who's got more drama coaches and make-up artists and speechwriters than Hollywood put together.

JIVE: More questions, Ladies and Gentlemen . . .
You, lady.

QUESTIONER #1 (*white girl, very timidly*): You've
done quite a bit of talking this evening and
I've found that you can be a very interesting
person. I wonder if you could tell me the most
exciting thing you've ever done.

BIG TIME: I guess the most exciting thing I did
was one night in North Korea in the woods
I raped a bear.

VOICE (*from the back*): What color was it?

JIVE: Oh, brother . . . More questions, please.

QUESTIONER #5 (*black man*): Why do you work
for a white producer?

BIG TIME: Why are we working for a white producer?

QUESTIONER #5: Isn't Zev Bufman white?

BIG TIME: Who is Zev Bufman?

JIVE (*to* QUESTIONER #5): He ain't at the meeting, dummy. (*To* BIG TIME.) Sorry, Big Time,
we gettin' them all tonight.

BIG TIME: Ask a question in context or we'll dump
you, boy.

JIVE: Do you want to ask a question or do you

103

want to be a smart guy? See that cat on the door, he's looking at your funny-looking head. Now, you want to ask a nice question, fella?

BIG TIME (*to* QUESTIONER #5): You may be confused, you see we . . . Jive . . . put "play" in the program instead of "meeting" because he didn't think as many people would come to a meeting as would come to a play.

JIVE: More questions.

QUESTIONER #5: Mister Big Time, it was mentioned before about Black Power. What will happen if this power is denied us in this country by the white power structure?

BIG TIME: Brother, if you don't know, if it ain't inside you . . . well, what can I say? (*He addresses the whole audience.*) Whether or not we're going to be free is not up to other people. If you think you'll be free, you know you got to be free, then you'll be free. It's really as simple as that and a system, a system that doesn't allow you to live like a man can't stop you from dying like a man, if it gets to that. What's going to happen, is that every black man is an angry man, even those who smile in your face, they don't like you. They smile, but they don't like you. They smile 'cause

104

they have to. You know that. You've created labels for them. Underneath them something different is happenin'. We all know that the label that covers the slow black man who doesn't seem to want anything, who's not inspired, so does just as little to get by, who's lazy—that label was created during slavery times when a black man worked sixteen to eighteen hours every day for nothing. And what that man was really doing was protesting or resisting the only way that was left for him to protest and resist. Now if we continue to be held down and tied to ghettos of hopelessness, then our anger is going to someday burst in an explosion and that explosion is going to unify all the colored people in the world. Colored people are seeing the white people's quest for power as a definite threat to them. I'm talkin' about people like the black people and the brown people and the yellow people and the red people and the disaffected, disillusioned white people, learnin' *how* to think and not *what* to think and lookin' at the system and saying it doesn't flow, this is not what it could be. They are making a black commitment. Now those white foxes can lean against grey doors of stone, contemplatin' Viet Nam and all those other irrelevant explosions. But if we have to we'll swipe your whole power

105

and snuff out your souls like cheap . . . birthday . . . candles.

RUBBER BAND: Ooooooeeee, Big Time talks some good shit! Run 'em on down.

WHITEY: What do you mean by "run 'em on down?"

HUNTER: Shut up, fool.

WHITEY (*to* HUNTER): If I want any more of *your* crap, I'll . . .

JIVE: What?

WHITEY (*to* JIVE): If I want any more of his crap, I'll rattle his cage.

ALL: Hey . . . hey . . . cut that out . . . hey . . . what you sayin' . . .

JIVE: You got somethin' to say, raise your hand.

WHITEY (*indicating* BIG TIME): I liked what he was sayin', but the rest of you, the rest of you just want to destroy everything. You're for destruction.

JIVE: What?

WHITEY: You're for destruction.

JIVE: Who is?

WHITEY: You is.

HUNTER: Tap the plate.

106

RUBBER BAND: You some sucker.

HONEY MAN: Some dude.

WEASEL: What business is you in?

HUNTER: Looks like he wants to train a Negro . . . Well, train me.

WHITEY: You think it is the color of a man's skin that makes him a man?

HUNTER (*pushes him down into his seat*): You sit down.

WHITEY: Who the hell do you think you're knocking down?

HUNTER: Go-liath!

RUBBER BAND: Get a Goliath . . . Little David here's gonna get a Goliath.

WEASEL: Might do it this summer.

WHITEY (*gets back up. Moves toward stage*): Now what about those thirty million Negroes you were talking about?

WEASEL: Thirty million! Shit . . . I know a million niggers myself.

RUBBER BAND: I know fifty million niggers in this country, at least, and they allllllll ready. No lie.

107

They all start to whoop it up.

WHITEY: Yeah, well why don't those fifty million niggers . . .

HUNTER, WEASEL, *and* RUBBER BAND *go after him.* WHITEY *retreats at a run up the aisle.* JIVE *and* HONEY MAN *try to get them back.*

JIVE *and* HONEY MAN: Weasel . . . Hunter . . . Come back here . . . Hunter, get back up here . . . Honey Man, get Rubber Band . . . Get back up here . . . Right now . . . right now . . .

They all return to stage. WHITEY *returns to his seat but remains standing.*

VOICE (*a young black girl, to* WHITEY): You shouldn't have ran.

WHITEY (*regains his composure*): We've heard guns and violence . . .

JIVE: What do you think this is . . . ?

WHITEY (*angry*): Well I just want you to be well aware that the white man will be ready for you next time and a lot of your black soldier boys will be getting it in the streets!

RUBBER BAND: I'm gonna get you first, Sucker!

BIG TIME (*calmly*): Look, mister . . . what I don't want you doing, what you is doing, coming up here and contaminating us—you're losin' your dignity. You losin' your dignity to machines, to war machines and destruction machines . . . You losin' the way your life should be lived . . . And you losin' what little you have left of love. We're standing here, we're naked but we've got our balloons. We've got big black balloons in our hands but the difference is we know what makes those balloons go, so, no more chains, 'cause we broke 'em once and we're gonna really get mad next time, and no more animals pullin' us with a plough, or slop slung at us, or feelin' a whip . . . Better not cry to your elusive god, he can't be no god. He can't even be no man. He lives just across the street, he lives at the same height as me, but he lives white. I'm gonna close the meeting.

WEASEL: You see, Whitey, you blow our minds with all that white dignity crap.

RUBBER BAND: Yeah man, you ought to become Albert Sweitzer.

HUNTER: GO TO AFRICA! There's a bunch of black people over there.

HONEY MAN: I forgot what Albert Schweitzer did?

WEASEL: He ran away to Africa and got himself dignity.

RUBBER BAND: He ran away to Africa and got himself some Ubangis, too.

BIG TIME (*his closing speech*): People seem to say that I preach a lot of hate, but I'll give you a little love to think on, before I leave. Think on a plant growing on three inches of earth. Now four times larger than the jar will grow the plant, yet that earth from where its life was fed will lose not a stone, will never change. The same three inches of earth. Well, that is the way that man's energy of compassion has always been, it's always been that, it will always be there, but it's always reached out and reached beyond, it's never been harnessed, but within, within from where that energy arose, that's the most powerful display of energy conceived. That's the kind of power that can change the events of time. That is the kind of power that can stop wars. That is the power that will create even more power. Will you ask history why then, with all that power, did a man kill a man? (HONEY MAN *helps* BIG TIME *with his cape.*) I know it's gonna hurt, but here we come. (BIG TIME *starts up the aisle.*)

ALL (*chant*): UHURU!!

110

BIG TIME: Bein' written on the wind . . .

ALL: UHURU!

BIG TIME: Bein' written in the flame . . .

ALL: UHURU!

BIG TIME: Bein' written in the ghetto . . .

ALL: UHURU!

BIG TIME: Bein' written by my black mama . . .

ALL: UHURU!

BIG TIME: It's bein' written by my black father . . . (*He leaves the hall.*)

ALL: YEAHHHHH!! Ain't that too much. WOW!!

RUBBER BAND: Big Time might be right, Jack, but it's too late for some of them Whiteys out there to learn.

HUNTER: Honey Man, it's just too late, Baby, it's just toooooo late, Man.

JIVE (*the businessman, back at his desk*): Well, it ain't too late for me. You know how much money we made here tonight?

HUNTER: It's a lean night, Jive.

JIVE: Well, don't show up here no more, none of ya.

111

RUBBER BAND: Hey, Man . . . I told you I don't play that shit.

ALL: You oughta be cool, Man . . . Yeah . . . Cut it out, Jive . . .

JIVE: Oh shut up!

WEASEL: Give out the money.

ALL: Yeah, let's go . . . the bread . . . yeah.

JIVE: I don't give out none of *my* money.

WEASEL: What you mean *your* money?

JIVE: My money. I'll take this money and spend it on me if I want to. You people make me so angry sometimes, I'm ready to take this money and eat and drink and . . .

HUNTER: Party!

RUBBER BAND: You better give me my share, Sucker.

JIVE: Honey Man, come here.

HONEY MAN: Yeah.

JIVE: Take this money and get some food, but get something special, a little different from the last time.

HONEY MAN: What've you got in mind?

JIVE: Some "chitterlings." (*All break up.*) Hey,

how many Brothers you know can get something as big as BAD off the ground like I did?

HONEY MAN (*smirks at everybody*): I don't know
any.

JIVE: That's what gets me so mad, when you people
don't understand what the facts are.

HUNTER: Now that you said that, give out the
money.

RUBBER BAND: Hey, Man, we know how good you
are, just go ahead and give out the bread.

JIVE: "Know how good you are . . ." If I am . . .

RUBBER BAND: We know how good you are.

JIVE: Rubber Band?

RUBBER BAND: Yeah.

JIVE: I want you to get the grass, Man.

WEASEL: Hey, Man, I want to get the grass!

JIVE: The last grass you got smelled like a Cuban
peed on it!

WEASEL (*starts to go*): I give up.

JIVE: Weasel, don't you give up . . . I want you
to get the wine, Brother. Weasel gets to get the
wine.

113

WEASEL (*returns*): Yeah!

JIVE: What kind of wine are you getting?

WEASEL: Napa-Sonoma . . .

WEASEL *and* JIVE: Mendo-cino Premium table wine.

They all crack up and WEASEL, RUBBER BAND *and* HONEY MAN *start out.*

HUNTER: Hey, you cats hurry up 'cause the party's gonna start early tonight.

HONEY MAN: Where we goin', Man?

RUBBER BAND: Back to Watts, where the hell you think?

HUNTER: Hey Jive, Big Time was too much tonight, wasn't he?

JIVE (*calculating finances with pencil and paper*): Sure was.

HUNTER: Yeah, but it should be (*He strides to the podium.*) BIG TIME BUCK HUNTER! That's right, I'll make things exciting.

JIVE (*preoccupied*): Hunter, come here.

HUNTER (*parading around*): Leave it to me. We'll *all* overcome. I'll make things a mess. Yes, I'll make them theatrical, I'll make them a musical. (*He hums and dances.*) Hum, hum, a hum hum.

114

JIVE: As of this minute, right now, we have a change going on, a whole new groovy change and it's got nothing to do with your musical.

HUNTER (*comes over next to* JIVE): A whole new change?

JIVE: A whole new change, so you best learn what it is.

HUNTER: I can't make no more new changes.

JIVE: Well, you don't even know what the change is.

HUNTER (*with mock interest*): Jive, what's this change called?

JIVE (*thinks quickly*): Innerism.

HUNTER: Jive, You've given me happy-ism, mysticism, militarism, and now you gonna lay on me . . .

JIVE: Innerism.

HUNTER: Sounds BAD.

JIVE: It *is* BAD.

HUNTER: I want to know how it goes.

JIVE (*like a used-car salesman*): Clasp your hands, Hunter. Close your eyes. Relax your body. Now let your mind wander, Hunter. Let your

115

mind go all the way back to the very beginning of The Hunter. Let it go all the way back to the womb, Hunter. Now feel! Feel, Hunter! Feel Innerism!

HUNTER (*he closes his eyes and hums*): Hmmmmmmmmmmmmmmm. Hmmmmmmm!

JIVE: . . . I think it's coming, Brother . . . Let innerism creep into the very marrow of your bones, Hunter! Innerism is the sun, the moon, and the stars. . . .

HUNTER: Hmmmmmmm . . . Hmmmmmmmmm . . . Hmmmmmmmmmmm . . . The sun, the moon, and the stars . . . Hmmmmmmmmm.

JIVE: *Innerism* is power, power, power . . .

HUNTER: Hmmmmmmmm . . . Power, power, power . . . Hmmmmmmmmmmmmm.

JIVE: Innerism is cosmic energy, Hunter . . .

HUNTER: Cosmic energy, Jive . . . Hmmmmmm . . . mmmmmmmmmmmmm . . .

JIVE: Innerism is a giant sexual orgasm . . .

HUNTER: Hmmmmmmmm . . . Hmmmmmmmmm . . . A giant sexual orgasm . . . HMMOOOO.

JIVE: Innerism is Beautiful Alleluiah Days.

HUNTER: Beautiful Alleluiah Days . . .Hmmmmm
mmm . . .

JIVE: Love, Hunter. It's love, love, love . . .

HUNTER (*Nirvana is approaching*): LOVE, LOVE,
LOVE . . . JIVE, JIVE!!

JIVE: Yes, Hunter?

HUNTER (*in total bliss*): SCOOBEEE DOOBEEE
DOOOO DOOOO DOOOO . . .

Lights fade out.

10167F
G